HUMPHREY DOERMANN

CROSSCURRENTS IN COLLEGE ADMISSIONS

*Institutional Response
to Student Ability
and Family Income*

TEACHERS COLLEGE PRESS

Teachers College, Columbia University

Acknowledgments

Many people have contributed to this book in one way or another; the few words said here represent inadequate thanks or acknowledgment, even for the most significant acts of assistance. These last must include the willingness of Wilbur J. Bender, Fred L. Glimp, Franklin L. Ford, and Gordon P. Gillis to encourage my outside-of-work interest in writing about the problems considered here, and to make time available to me for it. I wrote the first version of this book as a Ph.D. thesis. During that process I received the encouragement and perceptive criticism from three extremely helpful academic advisors at Harvard: André L. Danière, who gave me much time and assistance at critical periods, Theodore R. Sizer, and Arthur Smithies. Finally, three other members of the Harvard Faculty of Arts and Sciences offered particularly valuable help and comment: Dean K. Whitla, Seymour E. Harris (now at the University of California, San Diego), and David Riesman.

Although their specific contributions have also been acknowledged in footnotes to the main text, it should be noted here also that especially helpful unpublished data and analysis were given to me by Richard Dale Smith, Vice President and Registrar, University of Puget Sound, Tacoma, Washington; Walter M. North, Director, Office of Student Assistance, Knox College, Galesburg, Illinois; John M. Stalnaker and Robert C. Nichols, President and Director of Research, respectively, of the National Merit Scholarship Corporation, Evanston, Illinois; Henry S. Dyer, Vice President, Educational Testing Service, Princeton, New Jersey; and, at Harvard, by Fred L. Glimp and Dean K. Whitla.

Without special patience and encouragement at home over the better part of four years I would not have been able to complete this work; for these I owe special gratitude to my wife and daughters.

The errors in interpretation and execution which remain in the work are mine.

H.D.

Preface

For the past several years, trustees and administrators at private and church-related colleges, as well as many of their colleagues at public colleges, have known that costs of operation were rising uncomfortably rapidly compared with increases in their foreseeable sources of income. Early in the summer of 1967, Time Magazine made these concerns dramatic and public, suggesting that the nation's private colleges and universities are "in grave financial trouble" and that many "are searching frantically to close a dollar gap that threatens their very existence." [1]

A flurry of studies and proposals are in preparation for individual institutions and for the system as a whole, with the intention of helping to restore financial equilibrium and, one may hope, providing some financial margin for growth in the private sector and for improved quality of instruction. The income-expansion proposals which have been put forward so far range from those favoring more aggressive management of endowment portfolios (for the few colleges fortunate enough to have a portfolio to manage) to those suggesting that colleges sharply increase tuition rates, to those advocating greater state and federal assistance.

All of these developments, unfortunately, are happening in a marketplace about which surprisingly little is known. This study reports what one can discover after classifying each year's crop of high school graduates as follows: according to their measured scholastic aptitude and according to their ability (or rather, that of their families) to contribute financially toward college education. By seeing how these joint distributions change

---

[1] Education Section, *Time*, June 23, 1967, p. 78.

nationally from year to year and by comparing these shifts with similarly defined changes in individual colleges and groups of colleges, new trends and cross-trends become visible which were not apparent before. The results are disquieting. In important respects they are not what one might have expected before making the attempt. The study then applies these results to particular issues of student recruitment, financial aid, and institutional change faced by a number of private colleges, as those issues arise in the more complicated world that cannot be described by a two-dimensional table. The institutions providing the case studies are the University of Puget Sound, Knox College, Fisk University, and Harvard College. Against this background of market statistics and sampled experience, the study then considers, in ways which have received relatively little general attention, some of the underlying strains and pressures which already are at work. These help to determine how the structure of higher education may be forced to adapt, unless we explicitly choose different action.

One purpose of this book is to help college admission officers and administrators and trustees—particularly in the private colleges and universities—find ways to deal less uncertainly with a number of the operating questions they face each year: questions about admission standards, student recruitment policy, and tuition policy. Its potential value may be greatest for colleges whose immediate futures involve rapid change in these areas, and whose past experience, therefore, cannot readily be projected into the future as a reliable guide for operating decisions or as a guide for what consequences to expect next. The book is also intended for secondary school officials, legislators, government and foundation officials, and interested bystanders, and suggests which of the broadly related questions in the development of our colleges and universities now seem more pressing than had generally been thought. The questions seem urgent, and the time available to seek satisfactory answers seems unexpectedly short.

HUMPHREY DOERMANN
Belmont, Massachusetts
April 1968

Contents

List of Tables

I

Crosscurrents in Admissions
and Financial Aid

By late May, 1964, the dean of an Indiana boys' boarding school had received over twenty inquiries—some discreet, some not particularly so—from colleges anxious to know if any of the school's graduating students might still be looking for a college to attend in the fall. The dean could not remember a year when he had received as many letters of this kind, and from such good colleges.

At about the same time, the director of admissions at a good Illinois liberal arts college was discovering that his planned program to expand the student body was in trouble. Unless he lowered admission standards or sent recruiting letters to schools (he did neither), he could not meet his increased freshman enrollment target for the fall.[1]

These are surprising developments in a world conditioned by aggregate population statistics and by annual surveys in the national press to believe that each year more and more able students apply to more and more colleges of all kinds, and that entrance competition at all of these colleges is growing more intense and not less so.

From the end of World War II until the present, it has been true that a number of students graduating from high school each year in the United States has roughly doubled—from about one

million each year to more than two million. The proportion of
these students going on to college has also increased. Commonly
used estimates for future United States college enrollment foresee a doubling of the 1963–64 college student population by
1980.

INCREASED COMPETITION TO ENROLL
THE BRIGHT AND PROSPEROUS

Examples like those presented above deserve more attention
than they have received thus far, even though they seem to run
counter to the dominant pattern. While U.S. families have become more prosperous (better able to pay college expenses, all
other things equal), and have produced increasing numbers of
able sons and daughters, a significant number of U.S. colleges
and universities have been raising admission standards and raising the cost of attending them even more rapidly.[2] The net
effect, from the viewpoint of these colleges, has been to narrow
sharply the effective pool of applicants they can draw from,
even though the total college-bound pool is expanding.

For these colleges, which enroll a disproportionately large
share of the nation's future business and professional leadership
(presuming past patterns hold reasonably true in the near future), the effective applicant pools are now far smaller than is
generally acknowledged.[3]

Three years ago, for example, the directors of admissions of
the eight Ivy League colleges were asked to guess, for the year
1962, how many male high school graduates in the nation there
were who could score 550 or better on the verbal section of the
College Entrance Examination Board's Scholastic Aptitude Test
(SAT) *and* who also came from families with incomes of $15,700
or more a year. These two conditions described roughly (though
arbitrarily and incompletely) the minimum aptitude test scores
and minimum family incomes of the great majority of the full-
paying, nonscholarship freshmen in the Ivy League colleges that
year. The directors of admissions were being asked to estimate
how large a nationwide male candidate pool defined in these
joint terms, they thought they were drawing from as they se-

lected most of their full-paying, nonscholarship students. The admission officers guessed that the number of male high school graduates who could fulfill the joint specifications in 1962 was somewhere between 80,000 and 200,000 young men, with 100,000 the most common estimate. Further discussion of this illustration at the beginning of Chapter II will show that the actual candidate pool was much closer to 18,000 men, and in no case was it larger than 33,000, even after making every reasonable allowance for doubt. One could have selected somewhat different aptitude test score and family income boundaries and polled another group of informed practitioners, and the difference between informed guess and fact probably would have been as great.

Meanwhile, the competition to enroll students of high measured academic aptitude is growing more intense throughout a wide range of colleges. Any student who scores well enough on the National Merit selection test to become one of the nation's Merit Semi-Finalists may now expect to receive hopeful recruiting letters, sometimes a series of them, from about thirty different colleges. Private colleges which formerly drew students mainly from a local region have "gone national" in hopes of attracting more high-ability and, perhaps, full-paying students. The University of Denver, for example, a private institution, twelve years ago enrolled 80 percent of its students from an area that was within commuting distance. Today it enrolls roughly 80 percent of its students from outside the commuting area, and most of these from out of state. New Trier Township High School, an excellent public school in the prosperous North Shore Chicago suburb of Winnetka, Illinois, two years ago sent more of its graduates to the University of Denver than to any other single college.[4] At the same time, state colleges have established undergraduate honors colleges—both for their own educational worth, and also to help meet the increased competition for top students.

But while a few colleges have been able to enroll entering classes composed predominantly of high-aptitude students, many more colleges are now attempting to do likewise, and, given the relatively small supply of such candidates, it seems likely that most of these colleges will not succeed in their apparently well-intentioned attempt. The few colleges which do succeed, also, will have drained the pool dry—and will thus have affected their sister institutions far more than they imagined. For example, the eight Ivy League colleges in 1966 enrolled about 5025 male freshmen who scored 600 or better on the verbal aptitude section of the SAT. As Chapter II and Appendix A will explain, this number of freshmen represents about 16 percent of the male high school graduates in the nation who were probably able to score that well or better that year.[5] If all of the Ivy League colleges, rather than following their usual selection practices of recent years, had insisted on a *minimum* score of 600 on the SAT, and if each one of their 7500 male freshmen had thereby met this hypothetical requirement, that group of Ivy League freshmen would have represented about 24 percent of the nation's supply thus defined! It is this kind of sharp difference between what many colleges have thought to be their relationship to their market and what now actually appears to be the case that seems both interesting and of some concern.

THE DANGERS OF FRIENDLY COMPETITION

If the great competition should accelerate among colleges to enroll more and more students of high measured aptitude, it is then much easier to imagine a situation in which the colleges that lose in the competition may be forced to slow down their pace of study, while the colleges which win—if their student bodies are homogeneously high-testing and well-prepared—may wish to speed up the pace of their instruction. In the most selective colleges, also, the increased opportunity to choose often means increased opportunity, usually availed of, to reduce dropout. As dropout in these colleges decreases, their hospitality to transfer students from other colleges is also reduced, withdrawing another element of flexibility from the system as a whole. It is thus possible in the decade ahead that, without having agreed to plan it that way, the curricula, student academic capacity, and pace of study in our colleges could all become much more stratified than they have in the past. Should this be a source of worry? Perhaps not. But if the leading graduate schools in the nation in turn set their expectations of academic preparation by what they may expect from students coming to them from an emerging, fast-track group of colleges, and if these graduate school admission "expectations" gradually become minimum requirements, then it is possible to foresee our system of colleges operating far less flexibly than in years past as a system for sorting new talent into our society. Under the new conditions guessed at above, it may be increasingly important that applicants for the best starting jobs in many fields apply only after attending the "best" graduate schools, which in turn were accessible only after doing well in the fast-paced colleges. Much of the characteristic and important second-chance quality of our system of higher education could thus be in far more immediate danger than we have hitherto thought possible. Similarly, the opportunities to provide flexible and worthwhile new opportunities in higher education for disadvantaged minority groups may be seriously reduced, just when the nation is beginning to decide publicly that those opportunities should, if anything, be expanded.

Robert J. Havighurst, who has conducted some of the best available studies on the relationship between measured intelligence and socioeconomic status, has observed these forces at work in his studies, and comments:

There is a real threat to the maintenance of opportunity through higher education during the coming period of intense student pressure for college admission and greater selectivity on the part of colleges and universities.

Those most likely to lose opportunity are youth of working-class backgrounds who do not do especially well on scholastic-aptitude tests or in ordinary academic work, but who have a potential for college work that can be developed in a good college.

The tendency on the part of selective private colleges and universities to raise tuition fees to relatively high levels will have the consequence of driving more of the lower-status youth to the public-supported colleges.

The selectivity barriers, which will probably be raised even higher by the selective institutions, will tend to bring about more of a social stratification between high-status and low-status institutions.

Those of high status are in danger of becoming colleges for students of middle class origins, with small numbers of working class students. The low-status institutions may have to carry the main load of providing opportunity to students from lower-middle-class and working-class backgrounds.[6]

However, the second-chance, flexible quality, which has seemed in the past to distinguish American higher education from most European systems, has not only helped students from disadvantaged backgrounds or school programs towards a different kind of college and career experience, but it has also been significant for able students who have received better academic preparation for college than usual and who come from families with comfortable incomes. The majority of the National Merit Scholarship winners in the country could probably be described this way, and their changes in academic program and in career plans are therefore interesting. Dr. Robert C. Nichols, Director of Research for National Merit, reports that over two-thirds of the Merit Scholars appointed during the first four years of the program (1956 through 1959) made major changes in their career plans after they entered college, and 40 percent of the Finalists and Scholars in the 1956 competition changed their field of academic concentration between the summer before college and the end of sophomore year. If a number of the most selective colleges do enroll only the highest-testing students, and if these colleges do step up the pace of instruction in each of the major disciplines to the point where academic "shopping" becomes much more difficult in the time allotted, then the career penalties for students to change plans as these Merit Scholars did may become much greater than they have been previously. To the extent that these changing student interests are serious and worthwhile, their increased inhibition seems likely to be an obstacle to the best use of some of our most capable talent.

INCREASING FINANCIAL STRAINS

For many of the nation's private colleges, also, the most significant (and unhappy) *budgetary* finding of this study is that the national population of graduating high school seniors each year includes a surprisingly limited number of students who test high in academic aptitude and who also come from families prosperous enough to pay, unaided, the rising costs of private higher education. The varied definitions of "high-testing" and "prosperous enough" will be supplied later, with more evidence for the finding. The basic costs which a private college must meet in order to maintain and improve the quality of programs it offers continue to rise. If private colleges are more limited than they expected in their ability to raise the level of tuition fees without lowering academic qualifications for admission (which, oversimplified, is the clear implication of the earlier finding) the general pressure on their financial structure, reducing their ability to improve quality and variety of instruction, becomes greater than one might otherwise anticipate.

Furthermore, the total cost, principally in tuition, to students of attending private colleges and universities is rising more rapidly than that of attending public colleges. The competitive pressure upon the private sector is thus increased again, by steering into the lower-tuition public sector additional students who previously thought they could afford private college education. If these pressures accelerate the flow of new students into public colleges instead of private ones, it is an important financial and educational issue not only for individual private colleges, but for the taxpayers who will be called upon to pay the bill for sharply increased enrollment capacity in public higher education. As recently as 1950, half of the nation's college students were enrolled in private or church-related colleges. By 1965 the ratio of enrollment in private or church-related colleges to enrollment in public institutions was only one-third to two-thirds. Projections made by the Fund for the Advancement of Education in 1963 estimate that by 1985 the ratio may be something like one-fifth private to four-fifths public; to reach this position, ten additional students would be expected to register in public colleges for every one additional student in a private or church-related one.[7] In the states like California and New York, where particularly rapid change occurs, the difference between public and private sector growth rates could be even greater.

Whether this rapid a shift in balance is a good or a bad thing, or whether the issues of collegiate variety of control and purpose can even sensibly be discussed in these terms any more, are beyond the scope of this book. A few observers argue that we would suffer little loss if our whole system of higher education were publicly financed and publicly controlled, as university education is in many other parts of the world. If so, perhaps there is little point in raising the issue of balance between public and private control. But if there is an issue—and I believe there is an important one even though it has not yet been well defined—then it seems to merit more study and discussion than has yet taken place. The public Land Grant colleges, for example, made immense contributions in the development of applied technology and in community service at a time when the private college sector generally seemed to have other primary interests. Today, also, the public colleges and universities are accepting the challenge of trying to maintain and improve quality of instruction while they undergo unprecedented expansion of a kind the private sector has largely been unable to attempt. The private sector, on the other hand, has periodically set standards of quality which have influenced the total enterprise; in the 1950's, a few private colleges provided the leading edge of resistance to the excesses of McCarthyism, and so did much to preserve the health and morale of the whole academic community. There is little point in debating which sector has been of greatest value; the point is that each on occasion has helped the other in different but significant ways. Today in college admissions, two patterns predominate. In public colleges, students are usually admitted or not admitted depending on whether they attain a specified minimum high school record, a specified minimum set of aptitude test scores, or some combination of the two. In private colleges, particularly those with the opportunity to select a few from many applicants, the "objective" evidence of grades and test scores is often supplemented by teachers' and counselors' descriptions of style of performance, of energy and stamina and motive, and sometimes even estimates of future promise based on acquaintance and experienced instinct. These colleges then have the information to gamble, if they will, on qualities not solely measured by aptitude tests and transcripts. It would be difficult to argue convincingly that one system or the other ought to be adopted by everyone.   It would be just as difficult to argue that each does not possess its distinctive and useful features.   In the meantime it also seems clear that a general round of large tuition increases in private colleges, unaccompanied by offsetting new financial aid for students, can only accelerate the changing balance of public and private college enrollment within our present system—a change which is already proceeding at high speed, and is already creating major political strains within the states that have to provide for the greatest new tides of public college students.

Since this picture of shrinking candidate pools, decreasing flexibility in college admission patterns, and increasing financial strains is in sum more extreme than what is usually described in the national press or in the literature of college admissions, why should it only now begin to appear clearly?

MEASURING STUDENT FINANCIAL NEED AND ACADEMIC APTITUDE

For the greater part of the past three centuries, college administrators did not have available much reliable information as to the income distribution of college applicant (or enrolled) populations.   In most colleges it was considered poor taste to inquire regularly and directly of the families involved, and poorer taste still to attempt to verify.   In the early 1950's, however, the private colleges in particular felt increased pressure to extend the effectiveness of their scholarship funds in order to help cover student expenses which were then rising faster than they had for more than a century.   The College Scholarship Service in Princeton, New Jersey was founded in 1954 by a group of colleges to devise procedures whereby its members could inquire on a common basis about the family financial resources of their scholarship candidates.   These colleges could then tailor the size of scholarship awards to individual estimates of student financial need.   Some 500 colleges use these procedures today, including virtually all of the major private col-

leges and many public ones. Student loans provided under the
National Defense Education Act of 1958 also require the use
of a financial need appraisal, and have thus extended into many
other colleges the practice of inquiring about family finances
before awarding financial aid.[8] Scholarship awards to low-income students under the federal scholarship program of the
Higher Education Act of 1965 have extended further the practice of financial need appraisal.

Colleges therefore have a clearer idea than they did of the
family income distribution for those students who apply for
financial aid, although most have had little comparable information about families of students who do not apply for assistance.
But even the most prosperous colleges rarely give financial aid
(this includes loans and sometimes jobs as well as scholarships)
to as many as half of their undergraduate students; a recent survey by the College Scholarship Service suggests that roughly a
quarter of the nation's college students receive financial aid.[9]

Meanwhile, the College Entrance Examination Board's
Scholastic Aptitude Test did not begin to enjoy widespread use
until after World War II; only recently have colleges using these
tests been able to appraise with relative accuracy where their
admission standards intersect the national distribution of measured candidate aptitude.

Although direct evidence has been lacking about the incomes of the majority of United States college students, the
ones who do *not* apply for financial aid, one may still try to
appraise the financial strength represented at various ability
levels in the total national candidate group each year. By
treating family income (and from this, the ability of families to
contribute toward their sons' and daughters' college educations)
and measured scholastic aptitude as variables in a joint distribution problem, one can make a valuable, if approximate, analysis
of the size of different applicant pools which are defined by
different levels of student financial *and* academic ability. With
this analysis in hand, one can then appraise in a new way the
broadening or narrowing effect of changing admission standards
and financial policies by different institutions upon their student

bodies. Finally, one can also examine in a new way the national market for college education.

As long as the nation's colleges and universities operated at less than capacity, and as long as the major ones could enroll virtually all of the qualified students who applied for admission, the kind of appraisal suggested here could have had relatively little effect on institutional policy. The pressing question under those conditions was how to fill entering classes without unduly depressing entrance standards, not how to select from among many an optimum group, or spend much time thinking about various definitions of "optimum" and what their implications might be. Broadly speaking, United States colleges and universities have operated in a buyer's market from the American Revolution until World War II; only since then have seller's market conditions appeared for a significant group of institutions.[10]

Now we need to know much more about these changes. What are they doing to the structure and financing of higher education in the United States? How can individual institutions—particularly the private colleges, whose survival and growth depend so much on student willingness to pay relatively high tuition fees—appraise the direction and forces of change ahead of time, and so increase the chances of making workable and appropriate decisions about admission, tuition, and financial aid policy? How do the changing patterns of admission criteria and student charges and student financial aid affect the performance of students in college, and the distribution of talent after college in society? These are some of the important questions; yet they are so broad and complex that only the most able observers have thus far been able to give even partial answers which seem satisfactory. This study can set in place a few important elements and keep in mind the broader issues, but it will not attempt a comprehensive and nationwide review of them, even though such a review, if well done, would be of immense value.

Because, at first glance, the methods of analysis in the following chapter seem separate and even unrelated, it seems worthwhile to pause briefly to comment on some of the things each one does and does not propose to convey. The next chapter constructs a national set of estimates of the number of potential college candidates there were (or probably will be) in selected years from 1954–55 through 1974–75, who offer various levels of measured academic ability and also come from families with various levels of ability to pay for higher education. These estimates are derived through the joint distribution approach referred to earlier. In order to show the logic behind the estimates, how they were put together, and how they may be useful to individual colleges, the line of argument, briefly, is oversimplified: the pools of candidates which a particular college might draw from in the first illustrative examples are computed as if that college were concerned with attracting only full-paying students, and considering its tuition policy only in that light. Later examples derived from the recent experience of several colleges return to the reality of financially aided students and full-paying ones; but this first brief detour from reality can be bothersome without advance warning.

The joint distribution tables can themselves be bothersome at first encounter. They are constructed by using the two nationally available measurements (Verbal Scholastic Aptitude Test scores and family income) that seemed most appropriate for describing roughly the nation's male high school graduate population in terms of measured academic aptitude and of ability to pay for further education. (The joint distribution of female high school graduates for most purposes is similar, although the percentage of female students scoring well on verbal aptitude tests is slightly higher than the percentage of male students. Separate sets of tables have not been provided for female graduates.) Because the tables are important throughout the study, they are presented first and at some length, but it should not be assumed that this study has adopted the erroneous view that reported family income can be related precisely to the amount of money each individual student is able to and should be willing to devote to his further education, or that each student's Scholastic Aptitude Test scores measure accurately his total academic promise, regardless of health, attitude, judgment, socioeconomic background, or the appropriateness of the curriculum he selects. No such easy assumptions or conclusions are part of this study, and none such should be inferred from it.

MISSING DATA

This study is notably limited in the extent to which it tries to forecast further federal and state intervention in higher education and in the extent to which it tries to assist state and federal policymakers in deciding how government aid should be provided for college students in the future. This study did not judge these areas to be unimportant, nor did it assume these areas would undergo no change in the next ten or twenty years. The approach to the appraisal of federal and state scholarship, loan, and student work programs has been limited, surprisingly, by the lack of supplementary data.

The analysis of these issues might begin as follows, were the data available. From the joint distribution tables it is possible to estimate for each year's group of graduating high school seniors how much their families, in each major income bracket, might reasonably be expected to contribute for their sons' and daughters' college education. (One would have to estimate first how many students in each aptitude and family income bracket are not expected to continue their formal education.) From annual student expense budgets submitted for each institution to the U.S. Office of Education, and from available reports of student enrollment, it is possible also to estimate the aggregate annual college-going cost for these students and their families. But then the data become disappointingly inadequate. If one assumes that there are other pressing demands on state and federal budgets and that efficient spending for college student aid is important, one may also assume (granted that the assumption is debatable) that a major portion of our government student aid programs for undergraduates should have at least two characteristics: they should be designed to *supplement*, not replace, existing institutional and private student aid sources, and they should, where possible, be based upon apparent student financial need— so that prosperous students will not receive more than they need and low-income students will receive enough.[11] (These assumptions refer only to programs for undergraduate college students; major legislation for graduate student fellowships, assistantships, and traineeships already is proceeding under quite different assumptions.) If one is willing to set national goals to provide that a specified number of college students of appropriate academic qualifications have at least the economic opportunity to go on to college, then it ought to be possible to ask the following operating questions:

1. What is the aggregate financial need of these students? Aggregate need could be defined as the difference between the college-going costs they face and the resources they and their families can provide.
2. How much of this need is already being met from institutional and private (but not family) sources?
3. What, therefore, is the residual financial "gap" to be bridged by public funds if the original goals are to be met—and yet not overreached? This would be the gap between aggregate need (in 1 above) and that need already being met (in 2 above).
4. If this gap is to be bridged by public funds, what are the most appropriate ways of making them available: scholarship grants, loans, jobs, or some combination of the three?

Federal support for undergraduate student aid is already approaching half a billion dollars a year; surely these four questions are important. Yet to achieve sensible answers to the questions above one should know a number of things besides aggregate costs to students and aggregate student and family contributions to be anticipated. One should know, for a start, how the nation's high school graduates at present distribute themselves (by academic qualification and ability to pay) into the nation's colleges. If expensive colleges are attended only by the rich, and less expensive colleges solely by the poor, the cost of minimum supplementary financial aid would be substantially less than under conditions of considerable mixing of students. No census, from which such a student distribution can be known exists at present, although sample surveys are beginning to appear; the importance of this question is discussed at the end of Chapter II. If one had such census (or comprehensive survey) information available on a regular basis, one could then estimate periodically the changing answer to the first of the four questions posed above.

Unfortunately there is no census, or even a nationally reliable sample survey, to answer the second or third of the four questions in the detail needed. There are aggregate figures available as to the total institutional and governmental aid of various kinds being administered in different kinds of colleges, but the more complex task of determining how much of which kinds of aid—*in what combination*—are going *to which students who have how much financial need* has not been attempted. Yet without knowledge of these patterns, it is difficult to achieve a reliable yet broad view of where the important gaps are in our student aid structure, how big they are, and how they might best be filled in. The significant contribution this study could make to this set of problems must wait until these returns come in. One hopes it will not be too long.

One may also point out with reason that the discussion above applies principally to the support of students just out of high school in colleges that now exist in our system of higher education. It does not propose to deal with the different problems that would be raised if new kinds of institutions were to predominate, or if mature adults—no longer able to expect significant support from their parents—become a majority in the nation's undergraduate enrollment. Nor does it offer any alternate plan —hoped for by some observers—to solve the general financial problems of private colleges, not by a piecemeal approach (such as direct support for undergraduate financial aid), but by a system of institutional grants from public funds permitting a college to spend the additional money for student aid, library acquisitions, equipment, or salaries as it saw fit.

This study has been purposely limited in speculation of this kind, not because it is not important, but because the problems outlined previously, of understanding, operating, and expanding our present system, seemed to merit urgent attention of their own. New institutions, new patterns of post-high-school education, and new state and federal legislation will most certainly be part of the next ten years; if not, then the capacity of American higher education to meet new and much greater demands will be in serious danger. Nonetheless, my own judgment is that one of the distinguishing features of American colleges will continue to be the relatively large extent to which they are supported—to a greater extent than is true in other major educational systems in the world or in either pre-college or post-college education in the United States—by direct payments from students and their families. The majority of American college students in these years will most likely be men and women not long out of high school, even if the number and proportion of other students does increase. Finally, although public college enrollments seem likely to expand faster than private enrollments, I do not foresee the wholesale disappearance of privately controlled colleges nor the disappearance of separate admission, pricing, and student-aid practices in public and private colleges. These are, of course, debatable judgments, and they may prove to be embarrassingly incorrect; but if one does judge the future this way, then this book can be important to the problems of the future as well as to those of the present. The last chapter will conclude—as the first chapter began—with a plea for the design of new policies in admission, tuition, and student financial aid which promote flexibility, not rigid stratification, in the way students may distribute themselves throughout our system of colleges and universities.

Notes

[1] Humphrey Doermann, "Crosscurrent in Admissions," *Harvard Alumni Bulletin,* March 20, 1965, p. 460.

[2] There are probably between thirty and forty private colleges with selective admission competitions and with student expense budgets roughly similar to those of the Ivy League colleges (Brown, Columbia, Cornell, Dartmouth, Harvard, University of Pennsylvania, Princeton and Yale).

[3] For studies on the collegiate origins of men and women successful in various fields, see Robert H. Knapp, *The Origins of American Humanistic Scholars* (Englewood, N.J.: Prentice-Hall, Inc., 1964); Robert H. Knapp and Joseph J. Greenbaum, *The Younger American Scholar* (Chicago: University of Chicago Press, 1953); and Stanley C. Vance, "Higher Education for the Executive Elite," *California Management Review,* Summer, 1966, pp. 21–30.

[4] Information provided by Walden C. Irish, Director of Admissions, Univer-

sity of Denver, and J. William Gannoway, College Counselor, New Trier Township High School.

5 Information provided by Dean K. Whitla, Director, Office of Tests, Harvard University.

6 Robert J. Havighurst, *American Higher Education in the 1960s* (Columbus, Ohio: Ohio State University Press, 1960), p. 74.

7 Harold Wolozin, *The Outlook for Higher Education* (Washington, D.C.: Fund for the Advancement of Education, 1963), pp. 20, 21.

8 College Scholarship Service, *Financial Aid Manual: 1962–64 Edition* (Princeton, N.J.: College Entrance Examination Board, 1962), p. 1.   U.S. Senate, Subcommittee on Education of the Committee on Labor and Public Welfare, *National Defense Education Act of 1958, as Amended by the 88th Congress*, 88th Cong., 2nd Sess., 1964, Section 205, p. 21.

9 Elizabeth W. Haven and Robert E. Smith, *Financial Aid to College Students, 1963–64: Survey of Financial Aid Administered by Colleges and Universities to Full-Time Undergraduates*, Statistical Analysis Report, SR-65-15 (Princeton, N.J.: Educational Testing Service, March 1965).   Of 1700 colleges surveyed, 1221 reported that 132,455 of 677,048 freshmen (19.6 percent) enrolled in 1962 received financial aid administered by colleges and universities.   The colleges failing to respond were predominantly coeducational, small liberal arts colleges, and junior colleges, and predominantly located in southeastern United States.   It seems reasonable to assume that the nonrespondent institutions gave less aid per student to a smaller percentage of their enrollment than the national average derived from the respondent summaries.   This 19.6 percent figure for respondents in the survey refers only to aid administered by institutions of higher education. In addition, the College Scholarship Service estimates that almost 10 percent of the nation's students receive aid which is administered outside the colleges and universities.   Note that this definition of financial aid does not include the subsidy students receive, particularly in public colleges, because the tuition they pay is less than the cost of instruction received.

10 Frank H. Bowles, *Access to Higher Education*, Vol. I (Paris: UNESCO and the International Association of Universities, 1963), pp. 33, 34.   Frederick Rudolph, *The American College and University* (New York: Alfred A. Knopf, 1962), Chapters 9–13.

11 These assumptions, while defensible, are not the only ones which could be made.   Our Land Grant colleges, for example, developed for most of their history on the assumption that student aid, rather than being based on analysis of student (and family) financial need, should be based on a system of low tuition for rich and poor alike.   This is a much easier and neater system to administer, even though it may be less efficient in measuring and distributing subsidy more exactly where it is most needed and in the amounts needed.   Furthermore, if one assesses the American political climate differently one might assume that directing attention to *supplementary* government programs of direct aid to students represents an approach which is too limited in scope and which is outmoded.   Perhaps American voters and taxpayers will opt for rapid and massive government intervention, support, and control in all kinds of higher education rather than

choosing to operate as far as possible with more limited, supplementary aids. Political judgments of this kind, even if not explicitly stated, must precede any study of this kind, if only to identify problems which seem most significant to deal with. These political and environmental judgments are made explicit and discussed in the final chapter; in this introductory chapter it seems sufficient to acknowledge that they exist, that they are important, and that they are certainly debatable.

II

The Potential Student Market, Measured by Aptitude and Ability to Pay

Any system of higher education which, as in the United States, elects both to rely heavily on student fees and to place the control of policy at the institutional level then faces the question of how to set and to revise its student fee levels. This puts the matter too simply. In the United States, the "system" is an abstraction; the need to reach operating decisions about charges to students is faced more or less separately in the more than two thousand institutions of higher education throughout the nation. Furthermore, these decisions are really separate only in that it is the responsibility of the individual college or university to make them. The decision about what to charge students is often intertwined with questions of admissions and curriculum policy; who comes to a college may affect what can profitably be taught there. The decision, by definition, also affects the level of resources the institution can devote to instruction, financial aid, buildings, equipment, and so on.

WHY BOTHER TO EXAMINE THE MARKET?

This chapter will preserve much of the initial oversimplification as it proposes a new way of attempting to measure the market for higher education: estimating how many potential college candidates there are in any year (recent or near future) at various levels of measured academic ability, coming from families at various levels of ability to pay for higher education.

The setting of charges for dormitory space and food services will receive little attention here; in most public and private colleges these services are priced so that they will roughly break even. Other charges to students, particularly tuition, can raise more difficult problems. In theory a college, like any economic enterprise in a market economy, will do well to consider at least three elements in setting a price on its services: the internal costs of production; what the immediate competition is doing; and the customers' inclination and ability to pay. A single-purpose institution (a small liberal arts college, say, as opposed to a university whose faculty teaches graduates, undergraduates, and carries on research) may know its total costs. It may thus know its average cost per student—even though its accounting is not usually equipped to deal with the niceties of marginal cost (the cost of adding one more or a specific number more students). The multipurpose institution, the university, may not even know this much, without making unaccustomed estimates of the resources it devotes to functions like research which affect most college students only indirectly. Whatever the results of these attempts to determine costs, tuition rates can rarely be set which will cover full cost; rather, the immediate question is usually how much contribution students will be asked to pay toward an estimated full cost. Particularly among the private colleges and universities, a more powerful influence on pricing is a knowledge of what the competition is doing, combined with a usually great reluctance to get very far out of line.

Whether the resultant "herd" movement of tuition rates upward toward the also-rising cost level is appropriate and, in particular, whether it bears any relation to student inclination and ability to pay at various family income levels becomes an important question, yet one about which surprisingly little is known. "Appropriateness" will probably always remain a value judgment. However, a measurement which would indicate roughly how many students are likely to be able to fulfill various minimum measured aptitude conditions and *also* have available given levels of family financial support seems nonetheless likely to help appraise the direction and speed with which colleges change their hospitality to specific groups of potential students.

Any size-of-candidate-pool estimates of the kind underpinning this appraisal are bound to be arbitrary. Students are varied and complex enough, fortunately, to defy neat classification, particularly when the classification rests on only two variables: measured scholastic aptitude and ability to pay tuition and other costs. What, for instance, does a student have to demonstrate in order to be classified bright enough to do satisfactory work in college? That answer may depend in part upon aptitude test scores, but it also depends upon past performance, motive, and upon what a particular college may demand of him.

How can one know whether a student can command the resources to pay for tuition and other costs? Knowing the student's family income and its major financial obligations, and knowing the average full-cost student expense budget at particular colleges may help estimate the answer, but for any individual student the answer will still be imprecise. However, equally arbitrary and imprecise admission and scholarship decisions of this kind are made each year. Estimates of their aggregate shape are worth attempting even though these gross measures cannot be applied sensibly to predict individual performance or individual admission or scholarship decisions at particular colleges.

MARKET VARIABLES: MEASURED APTITUDE AND FAMILY INCOME

Two crude variables will serve for these estimates: one for brightness, one for prosperity. In this section, for simplicity of argument, the measures will be applied only to the Harvard College admission situation. The arbitrary cut-off points selected for the first example are the same as those used in the poll of the Ivy League directors of admissions, described in Chapter I. However, by changing the cut-off levels one selects for student brightness and prosperity, one can consider any college in the United States.

Measured aptitude

The verbal score on the College Entrance Examination Board's Scholastic Aptitude Test will serve as the measure of brightness. If one is to choose a single measure from the many which are actually used to try to appraise academic promise in a candidate, the SAT verbal score seems the most promising for aggregate analysis. It is a reasonably valid predictor of aggregate performance (although performance in secondary school measured by rank-in-class seems to be more valid), and it is the only nationwide academic measure of Harvard's candidate group (and of many other colleges) scored on a common and comparable basis. If an admission candidate in his senior year in high school scores below 550 on the verbal section of the SAT, the Harvard Committee on Admissions and Scholarships will look particularly carefully for other positive evidence of academic promise before guessing that he can do the necessary work without undue difficulty. In practice, about 8 percent of the recent freshman classes in Harvard College have scored below 550. A follow-up study conducted by the Harvard Office of Tests as of June 1964 inquired about the performance of 1165 freshmen who had registered six years earlier, in the fall of 1958. It showed that 88 percent had graduated, and that about half of those who graduated did so with honors. Of the 132 freshmen who had scored between 340 and 550 on the verbal section of the SAT, 93 percent had graduated, about one-third of the graduates having attained honor records, and of the 306 freshmen who had entered with verbal scores above 700, 90 percent had graduated, about two-thirds of the graduates having attained honor records. These performance results should not imply that the lower a man's verbal SAT score, the more likely he is to graduate from college, nor should they imply that the SAT is a worthless predictive instrument. The meaning, taken in context, is that other things besides test scores are important in determining individual performance and that the Harvard Committee on Admissions and Scholarships has tried to take account of them—particularly when it gambled on the probable performance of the lower-scoring men.

National norms for the SAT

The scoring range of the Scholastic Aptitude Test starts at 200 (low) and extends to 800 (high) with the median of those taking the test each year roughly 500. Since the test is predominantly taken by those who intend to go on to college, further adjustment is necessary before one can estimate what proportion of a broader population would probably be able to score above given levels. In 1960 the Educational Testing Service administered the Preliminary Scholastic Aptitude Test (similar to the SAT but one hour long instead of three hours) to the complete senior class in a representative national sample of 200 secondary schools selected from a list of the 23,655 public and non-public high schools in the United States. From the results of this, Educational Testing Service estimated that the following percentages of all United States male high school seniors would be able to achieve at least the following Scholastic Aptitude Test verbal score levels.[1]

SAT verbal score	Percentage of male high school seniors likely to score this well or better, as estimated by ETS
650	1%
600	3%
550	9%
500	15%
450	24%
350	50%

The 1960 survey by Educational Testing Service forms an important part of the estimates which follow in this study; its major advantages and limitations for this purpose merit comment. Since 1941 the designers of the Scholastic Aptitude Test have attempted to calibrate this instrument so that, even though the actual questions asked do change from one edition of the test to another, a particular score still connotes the same level of accomplishment: a verbal score of 500 in 1955 should imply the same verbal aptitude as a verbal score of 500 in 1965. This procedure has important advantages. College admission officers and curriculum designers are able to see, over the years, how the measured aptitude of their particular constituencies is changing and to see this without further calibration or adjustment of the scores achieved by their applicants or enrolled students.

It is not known, however, how the *proportions* noted above from the 1960 study are changing over time. Is the proportion of high school seniors who are able to score 500 (or better) increasing, holding constant, or decreasing? A new benchmark survey has been started by Educational Testing Service, but the final results are not yet available. A number of forces seem to be at work which will affect the results. Federal programs, state programs, and individual school districts have been attempting to develop ways which will encourage a larger proportion of each age group not to drop out of school, but to graduate. All other things held constant, the effect of this should be to increase the proportion of middle- and low-aptitude students represented in graduating senior classes. Meanwhile, however, the general quality of instruction in our elementary and secondary schools is improving, and students in many schools are being offered more sophisticated material earlier in their school careers. Since aptitude tests measure not only hereditary endowment but accomplishment as well, the effect of generally improved instruction should be to improve generally the scores achieved by graduating seniors—since the calibration of what each aptitude score level means is designed to be constant.

What the net effect of these two offsetting pressures will be is difficult to forecast. For want of firm data, it will be assumed, for the estimates in this study which follow, that the offsetting pressures are about equal in magnitude, and that the proportions noted above for the 1960 survey may therefore be applied back to 1955 and forward to 1975. However, the further away one works from 1960, the more one should bear in mind the possibility of significant error in estimating. It is conceivable, for instance, that by 1975 the percentage of high school graduating seniors likely to be able to score 500 or better on the verbal section of the Scholastic Aptitude Test could be as high as 25 percent—instead of the 15 percent who probably could have done this well or better in 1960. The shift may not be this great, or it may take place unevenly and in the lower portions of the scoring scale. This element of uncertainty is borne in mind throughout this study and does not seem to damage significantly the major conclusions; it does remind one again, however, that the new estimating procedures proposed here are rough ones, not precise ones.[2]

Aggregate versus individual measurement

One should also differentiate between the use of test scores in aggregate measurement and in individual cases. While the table of proportions above probably is an adequate gross estimate of measured aptitude levels in the national population designated, considerable variation occurs in individual score patterns. The test scores for an individual student on successive testing days may be expected to vary as much as 60 points, even though the test-taker is equally healthy and alert on the two days and is trying equally hard to do his best. Also, nervousness or unfamiliarity with multiple-choice test forms may cause still larger individual variation from the score level which would ordinarily most accurately predict ability to do college work. Although one may suspect that the racial and socioeconomic background of a student also affects the relationship of his Scholastic Aptitude Test scores to his later college performance, the available research is, in part, conflicting and certainly incomplete.

If this aggregate analysis were for only a single measured variable, measured academic aptitude, the discussion could end here. One could multiply the total number of male high school graduates times the desired percentage factors from a brief table like the one above, and arrive at rough candidate-pool estimates for various kinds of men's colleges. (With women's test performance figures, or combined figures, similar estimates can be worked out for women's or coeducational colleges.)

Harvard College in 1962, for instance, chose more than 90 percent of its entering class from a national pool of about 85,000 male high school seniors who were able to score 550 or better on the SAT. (Multiply 941,000 male high school graduates for 1962 times the 9 percent who are probably able to score 550 or better.) Ten years earlier, 90 percent of the entering Harvard College class came from a pool of about 114,000 men scoring 474 or better. This kind of rising-score, shrinking-pool trend has occurred at many colleges across the country, and at virtually all of the ones which have had increasing opportunity to be selective in admissions.

The one-variable analysis, while perhaps of some interest taken alone, understates the amount and speed of change occurring in effective candidate pools both in the selective colleges and elsewhere. Addition of the prosperity variable to the analysis yields neither precision nor, along with measured ability, accounts for all of the change which is taking place; it does, however, seem to alter the results significantly enough to be worth the added effort.[3] Before attempting to combine the two variables in different ways, it seems worthwhile first to examine the prosperity variable briefly by itself.

Family income and the ability to pay for college

One may illustrate the specific case by asking: How many male students in the nation are prosperous enough to pay tuition and other costs at Harvard College without scholarship aid? (Note that this particular illustration inquires only about the pool of candidates who could attend *without* financial aid. The relationship between the pools of full-paying potential candidates and of aided ones for a college is dealt with later.) Harvard College and some 500 other colleges attempt to answer the question for individual students by using the general approach and the procedures recommended by the College Scholarship Service. Depending on a family's income and assets and upon major obligations against that income and borrowing power, the College Scholarship Service has worked out ways of estimating how much the family might reasonably be expected to contribute toward a son's college education. If one of the participating colleges decides to award him a scholarship, its financial aid officer calculates the amount of the award by subtracting the amount the family is expected to contribute from the college's full-cost (including allowance for personal expenses) student budget.[4]   In many cases the college will also subtract, during this calculation, a further amount: the student's own contribution from job earnings or from taking a loan.   The remaining financial gap is the size of the scholarship which the student is offered.

A normal-budget, three-child family at an average distance from Cambridge, Massachusetts in 1962 was considered able to meet the Harvard student budget, barely, if its income was about $15,700.   At this income level or higher, the "normal" family was deemed *not* in need of supplementary financial aid. Again, although a simplified aggregate picture may be described with these particular figures, the individual scholarship applicant whose families are "normal" in all the above respects is rare indeed; hence the cut-off line between need and no-need varies from family to family.   Furthermore, although the College Scholarship Service procedures seem to have worked out satisfactorily in general, no one claims that they equalize precisely the actual financial strain of helping to support a son on scholarship in Harvard College.

The aptitude and income variables combined

There are a number of possible ways to combine the aptitude and family income percentile estimates to try to find out how many male high school graduates in the nation could have probably scored 550 or better on the Scholastic Aptitude Test *and also* came from families which earned $15,700 or more in 1962.   One way is to assume that only rich families produce sons who score particularly well on aptitude tests.   This assumption would produce the largest pool which could meet or exceed both conditions.   In 1962 it would have been about 85,000 men: 941,-000 male high school graduates times the 9 percent who could score above 550.

Another approach is to suggest that no relationship exists between family income and student aptitude test performance. If family income and student aptitude test performance were independent variables, then one would calculate an available pool of about 10,000 men. This arises from the calculation: 941,000 times 9 percent (the aptitude probability) times 12 percent (the income probability).[5] These two approaches seem to define the reasonable limits to the question. The more closely and positively family income percentile levels and offspring test score percentile levels are correlated, the larger the size of the pool one estimates for these particular associated aptitude and income probabilities, up to 85,000.

A national study of the relationship between student aptitude and family income has not been undertaken. Smaller studies have been done, however, using measures other than the Scholastic Aptitude Test, and using socioeconomic classifications other than family income. Eells, Davis, Havighurst, Herrick, and Tyler have summarized the research between 1900 and 1950 on the correlation between socioeconomic status and intelligence test scores and found it to be generally in the neighborhood of 0.35. One of the largest recent studies was conducted by Eells, who administered five different intelligence tests to 5000 nine- and ten-year-olds and thirteen- and fourteen-year-olds in Rockford, Illinois schools. Depending on the test, the correlations between socioeconomic status and intelligence test scores ranged from 0.20 to 0.43.[6]

Although income is closely associated with socioeconomic status, and by some definitions may be explicitly included, the significant published research in this area has used other measures than income for classifying socioeconomic groupings. Thus the research described above, while apparently relevant, is not directly transferable to the present study.

Some corroborating empirical evidence comes, however, from the National Merit Scholarship Corporation in Evanston, Illinois. This organization tested approximately 800,000 juniors and seniors during 1964. The selection of the final National Merit Scholarship winners involves first selecting (by aptitude tests) an intermediate group of semifinalists; in 1964 this semifinalist group numbered 14,000. While the test score cutoff point for the semifinalists varied from state to state, the national average cutoff score was equivalent roughly to an SAT test score of 636. (Thus the National Merit cutoff was a more demanding one; intersecting the top 2 percent of measured ability in the male high school senior population, instead of the top 9 percent suggested by the 550 SAT score example.)

In addition, National Merit asked whether the students tested needed financial aid in order to attend college, and if so, what the amount of their family's federal income tax payment was for the previous year. By adding together those who reported federal income tax payments in excess of $2500 (in normal-budget, three-child families prior to the 1964 tax cut this corresponded to roughly a $15,000 income or more) and those who felt they would not need financial aid (whose families were presumed to be earning $15,000 or more—even though a few lower income families might be incorrectly included), it was estimated that the number of semifinalists whose families earned more than $15,000 the previous year was roughly 5000. John M. Stalnaker, President of the National Merit Scholarship Corporation, estimates that his program tests a majority (how great a majority is not known) of all U.S. seniors able to achieve semifinalist-level test scores. Using this single-pool estimate to check against the calculations in Appendix A (which is discussed more fully below), it seems as if a correlation coefficient of 0.4 between family income and test scores is a reasonable degree of linkage, although not the only possible one, to establish for these estimates.[7]

Returning to the Harvard College example, and using a coefficient of 0.4, one can calculate that in 1962 the number of male high school graduates in the nation able to score better than 550 on the SAT *and* whose families earned $15,700 or more was about 18,000.[8]

In many ways, the tables which form Appendix A are important to this study, and hence their use deserves some explanation here, even though the general logic behind them has just been discussed and the technical elements of their construction are treated in a note at the end of Appendix A. The cells of the 1961–62 table (see page 133) which determine the 1962 Harvard College probable candidate pool in the example above are shown below with the necessary interpolation.

Pool of candidates having SAT scores of 550 (1961–62)

Family income percentile level (head of family aged 35–64)	Family income and possible family contribution for college (in parentheses)	Estimated number of male high school graduates from families with these incomes, low and high estimates
85	$14,000 ($2350)	21,000 37,000
88	**$15,700** *	**18,000** * **31,000** *
90	$17,100 ($3380)	16,000 30,000

* Figures set in boldface obtained through linear interpolation.

In the actual table, one locates the column for the minimum SAT score of interest, 550 (which is also the 94th percentile of measured aptitude for male high school seniors in the nation), and the row for $15,700, the minimum family income of interest (for a "normal"-budget, three-child family), which must be arrived at by interpolation, since the table only shows candidate pools for family incomes at the 85th percentile level in the nation ($14,000) and at the 90th percentile ($17,100).[9] The figure in parentheses immediately below the family income is the College Scholarship Service dollar estimate of the average family contribution possible for college education for a year—associated with that level of income. (It would, of course, be possible to start in the table with this figure instead.) In each of the resultant cells (at the right) is a pair of numbers, each number being an estimate of the number of male high school graduates in 1962 who meet or exceed the marginal conditions specified. The smaller figure in each pair results from using a correlation coefficient of 0.4, which seems to be the most reasonable estimate available. In the high ranges of income and measured ability, the pool estimates seem surprisingly small. The bottom figure in each cell is therefore calculated using a coefficient of correlation of 0.7—which is probably too high but is included to illustrate the largest reasonable estimate of the candidate pool. In either case, the pool estimate seems surprisingly small—even when the error in the distributions and the doubt introduced by the uncertain degree of correlation are considered; it would not be surprising to discover the pool size actually five or ten thousand men larger or smaller than the estimate calculated. Even admitting this degree of uncertainty, the results seem significant because the pool of candidates emerges so unexpectedly small at this high level of student ability and family income. (Those who are interested in the mathematical assumptions and procedures employed in constructing the bivariate normal distributions which underlie the tables in Appendix A should turn to the *Notes* following those tables, beginning on page 146.)

This kind of statistical exercise is of interest because it permits assessment of the market for college education in ways not possible before, ranging across some of the most important admission, tuition, and financial aid policy questions which face individual colleges and groups of colleges. Moreover, if other supplementary data become available, this kind of measurement could help evaluate the adequacy or inadequacy of government financial aid programs for students in ways which seem extremely desirable but which are not now possible.

THE UNIVERSITY OF PUGET SOUND APPRAISES ITS MARKET

For an example of how this kind of measurement applies to an individual college, consider the experience of a Methodist-founded coeducational college, the University of Puget Sound in Tacoma, Washington. In 1960 the university enrolled 480 freshmen students. Tuition was $600. Over 90 percent of these freshmen students were from the State of Washington and more than 65 percent commuted from home. This was the first year in which rising tuition costs had reached the point where it was as economical for Tacoma students to go out of town to a state college as it was for them to commute to the University of Puget Sound.

In order to meet the increasing competition of the public institutions of the state, the University of Puget Sound embarked on an overall plan to improve its academic offerings, faculty salary scale, student services, and academic aptitude of the admitted students, and to expand its enrollment. Up to and including the 1964–65 academic year, the ambitious plan met with remarkably consistent success. Although in 1962 a new junior college opened twenty miles away and in 1963 tuition rose to $1000 and the median SAT score (both Verbal and Mathematical) had risen nearly 100 points between 1958 and 1965, the expanding enrollment targets were met in every year but the last. (During this same period the average grade point average of the entering class had also risen nearly 0.4 of a grade point, on a scale of 0 to 4.0, and in the last year the grade point average and SAT results enjoyed the largest one-year increase in the university's history.) The 67 percent increase in tuition charges, meanwhile, had made possible a 40 percent increase in faculty salary levels.

In admissions there was not much margin to spare, however; the University of Puget Sound admits approximately three-fourths of its applicants. In order to meet the expanding enrollment targets (the entering class in 1965 had increased to 550 students), the Admissions group had expanded from one person, in 1958, to three full-time and four part-time staff members. What the staff recruiting accomplished was little short of a revolution. Admissions staff visits to high schools, first limited to the State of Washington, were extended into Oregon and then urban California, then Denver and the north shore suburbs of Chicago, then Houston and Dallas, Texas. Admissions visits to the East Coast were planned for the fall of 1966. By 1965, 40 percent of the entering class came from out of the state, and of the 60 percent from Washington only about a third lived within commuting distance. Students from low-income homes in Tacoma and elsewhere enrolled less and less frequently and were replaced by students from more prosperous and sophisticated suburban families.

In 1965 a public junior college opened in Tacoma. This was the first year that the University of Puget Sound had not quite been able to meet its enrollment expansion plan. The university had survived unexpectedly severe competition remarkably well, although to do so it had been forced to move into direct competition for students in many areas where Methodist-founded colleges already existed and were facing similar pressures: something clearly not anticipated by the founders. The university also faced a rapidly expanding state system of higher education and intensified admissions recruitment on the part of all of other major private colleges in the Pacific Northwest. With one revolution accomplished in student admissions, the pressures of competition, while different now and perhaps more complex, seemed no less intense in 1965 than in 1960. Should the University of Puget Sound admissions policies continue along the same paths set in the 1960 to 1965 period or did some modification seem advisable? These questions were in the mind of the Vice President (the former Director of Admissions and Registrar) of the university when he inquired what the tables described in this chapter could tell him about the choices the institution faces now. He wrote:

Assume the SAT upper score limit of the lowest decile in the admitted freshman class is about 400 and the total resident budget is $2250. What is the reservoir of available students? What happens to it if tuition and fees are raised $200? What happens if that 10th percentile SAT score level is raised 50 points, and what happens if both of these steps are taken simultaneously? [10]

From the 1964–65 table in Appendix A one can calculate the answers in the manner described above for the Harvard College example, except that since University of Puget Sound draws both men and women students, the pool estimates (calculated in the tables for male students only) should be doubled to yield an adequate set of approximations here.

The 1965 candidate pool for the University of Puget Sound

is roughly 464,000 male and female high school graduates. If in 1965 the 10th percentile score level had remained at 400 but tuition were raised $200, the pool would have been 418,000, a shrinkage of 10 percent. If the tuition had remained unchanged but the 10th percentile score level had been moved up to 450, the pool would have been 316,000, a shrinkage of 32 percent. If both steps had been taken at once, the pool would have been 288,000 students, or a shrinkage of 38 percent. With other elements affecting students' decisions to apply to the University of Puget Sound, and to enroll if admitted, remaining constant, any of the suggested admissions or tuition policy changes would therefore make it more difficult to meet enrollment requirements. The relative degrees of added difficulty are suggested by the different percentages of shrinkage in the potential candidate pools calculated from Appendix A. Note that this would not necessarily be true for a college admitting only a small portion of the candidates that seem qualified.

One should, of course, treat such estimates with caution. Although the linkage between a reduction in pool size and recruiting difficulty seems reasonable, untested assumptions are involved in making it. Also, all the other elements never do hold constant. This exercise says virtually nothing of the quality of academic or extracurricular life in the institution, how it is changing, and how well known those changes are among prospective candidates, yet these matters are critically important, although extremely difficult to measure. On the other hand, these estimates provide a kind of advance warning not previously available, which can help predict the direction and rough magnitude of enrollment pressures before institutional policy has been committed to opposing them or running with them.

KNOX COLLEGE: A LONG-RANGE PLAN IS REVISED

Knox College, an independent coeducational liberal arts college in Galesburg, Illinois, provides another example in which the joint distribution tables discussed at the beginning of the chapter help one to understand the problems faced by an institution as it tries to grow and improve in quality. Since Knox, earlier than most similar colleges, projected a long-range budget plan to set a benchmark for its overall growth, it is possible to compare the initial plan with later results and inquire as to the major reasons for the difference. One should not infer that because the results *were* different, the policymakers at Knox were either shortsighted or foolish. The opposite conclusion is much closer to the truth. By setting forth ahead of time what seemed to be a reasonable budget view of the future which also seemed consistent with other operating policies, by making careful inquiry later as to why the budget and the actual experience seemed to be moving apart, and then by revising operating policies (and also revising the projected budget plan) the college placed itself in a far healthier position than many otherwise similar colleges to respond intelligently to its environment and to its changing opportunities. Meanwhile, the availability of the initial budget plan makes it possible to illustrate not only how one may better understand a college's admission, tuition, and financial aid problems, but also how important these questions are to the overall development of the institution and its long-run financial health.

In 1959, Knox's president, Sharvy G. Umbeck, with some of his colleagues at Knox, and Sidney G. Tickton, Program Associate for the Fund for the Advancement of Education, assembled for the college a long-range plan which was to have significance for Knox College and for scores of other colleges—principally private colleges—throughout the nation. The ten-year plan, with a description of how it was constructed, was published as the "Ashford College Case" and read widely by college administrators and trustees.[11] It then was used as a college-management training device by the Fund for the Advancement of Education, which sponsored more than two hundred long-range planning seminars during the following three years using the case as the basic framework within which the participating institutions supplied and then debated their own different data, assumptions, and goals for the future.[12] Finally, between 1960 and 1964 the Ford Foundation embarked upon an ambitious program of development grants to selected private universities and colleges; during this period the Ford Foundation granted more than 200 million dollars to forty-seven private liberal arts colleges, ten universities, and thirteen predominantly Negro colleges, to cite their categories.   In order to receive serious consideration by the Ford Foundation for the award of one of these development grants, a college was usually expected to complete a self study and long-range plan.   This, in turn, usually included a projection of the kind used in the Ashford-Knox case.[13]   By 1964, among a sizeable group of college and university financial officers, the Tickton Method had become a byword.

The Tickton Method

The Tickton Method, for which Knox College provided the first and best known example, is not entirely new.   For some time before 1959, American businesses had been using similar methods to forecast cash budgets and problems of corporate expansion.   Colleges and universities had also built projection models to help plan development and change, but the Tickton Method was unusual in that so great a number of institutions, hitherto unaccustomed to overall or long-range budget planning, so quickly took it up and took it up seriously.   The Tickton Method requires, first of all, self-examination and a collection of internal statistics, with particular attention to the following detailed statistics of the prior ten years.

1. Enrollment figures.
2. Number of students housed and fed by the college.
3. Number and percentage of students receiving scholarships and loans.
4. Geographic origins of students.
5. SAT scores and high school class rank statistics.
6. Charges to students for tuition and fees, for room and board.
7. Number of degrees granted.
8. Number of students enrolled with national scholarships (for example, National Merit, Sloan, and so forth).
9. Percentage of graduates going on to postgraduate education. Number who receive national awards at graduation from college (for example, National Science Foundation Fellowships or NDEA Fellowships).
10. Number of full-time equivalent teaching faculty at each level, and

their average and total compensation—including appraisal of fringe benefits.

11. Number of students per faculty member.
12. Balance sheet and annual operating statement information.
13. Sources and applications of new money (in addition to tuition and endowment income) received.

The approach then requires making a series of assumptions about the ten-year future: first, about the national and international environment—for example, that there might not be a global war sufficient to seriously disrupt the normal flow of students wishing a college education, or that the nation would somehow avoid a major depression; then, about the demand for the particular kind of education the institution expects to provide; and finally, about the elements in the list above—the internal elements that help translate institutional purpose in the national environment into some workable outline of operating and budgeting practice. The assumptions are then costed out, and if income and expense do not match, the initial assumptions must be changed as painlessly as possible until the two elements do come together. The principal virtue of the Tickton Method is that it generates a simple yet comprehensive framework within which assumptions about income and expense and assumptions about institutional size and balance must be put together consistently. If the assumptions are not internally consistent, the results show it quickly. On the other hand, like many models, it oversimplifies: it cannot generate its greatest value for planning unless it is reinforced both by well-informed appraisal of the external environment and by considerable knowledge of the content, form, and style of teaching and learning that has gone on before, and a knowledge of that which, ideally, should take place in the period ahead. Without this kind of background, it is possible to generate an internally consistent set of projection figures, but they either will not work at all, or they will not work without generating excessive internal friction. With this kind of background, however, the Tickton framework can illustrate the reasonable consequences to the future budget that result from costing out the best-available present assumptions, and it can also help isolate areas of particular financial stress or leverage for further study.

No one claims, Tickton least of all, that a projection of this kind should be adopted by a college as a fixed, inflexible, year-to-year operating plan, or that it should become a standard by which future institutional "success" or "failure" is measured. To permit this would risk ignoring unforseen opportunities or problems when they arise. Construction schedules, for example, may need revision when donor plans change unexpectedly. If the nation were to enter a severe economic depression, it might be disastrous to execute a previously planned schedule of tuition increases which had been made up under a no-depression assumption. These are examples purposely made extreme to provide some perspective for the Knox example.

The Knox long-range plan

The 1959 Tickton projections and the operating results finally achieved by Knox College in 1963–64 were similar to each other in some respects. A few of the differences seemed to result from overoptimistic assumptions in the original projections about the supply of academically able, also prosperous applicants, but the other important differences were the result of alert annual revision of spending priorities and of operating plans following the review of recent past experience and newly appearing opportunities.

The comparison does show that changes in tuition rate, changes in student recruitment, and changes in student financial aid policy are intimately related to the college's overall budget, that unexpected change in one or more of these elements may greatly affect the others. It fails to show the effect of the process of annual review that took account of many of these changes as they developed. For example, the college consciously elected to recruit and enroll more needy but able students, who were located by the new Illinois State Scholarship Program. Fund-raising efforts were diverted from endowment (for scholarship and other purposes) to the newly generated, larger expenses of student financial aid. The college consciously chose to admit these more "expensive" students rather than many less able students who did not require financial assistance. When enrollment in a particular year turned out to be somewhat smaller than had been expected, the effort to solicit current-use gift monies was increased, in compensation for the loss of tuition income.

The original Tickton projection was an ambitious one. Following are five of the major elements of the plan, which initially was to run from 1958–59 to 1967–68.

1. Increase student enrollment in the college from 800 to 1250 by 1963–64, then stabilize at this level to 1967–68.
2. Increase the total number of full time faculty members from 70 to 89, or 27 percent, during the ten-year period.
3. Increase the average salary per faculty member from about $6000 in 1958–59 to $9190 in 1963–64 to $11,172 in 1967–68. Increase fringe benefits, as a percentage of salary, from 7.9 percent to 15.75 percent.
4. Increase tuition and fees for students from $817 in 1958–59 to $1525 in 1963–64 to $1841 in 1967–68. Meanwhile, raise significantly the ability level of entering classes. Increase the percentage of enrolled students receiving scholarships from 47 percent in 1958–59 to 52 percent in 1963–64 and stabilize at that level.
5. Expand and improve the educational plant and related facilities.[14]

Elmer F. Jagow, Treasurer and Business Manager at Knox, reported on the results of the first four years of the plan to the 1963 College Scholarship Service Colloquium in Excelsior Springs, Missouri:

The students are better academically than they used to be, the average College Board Scholastic Aptitude Test Score having jumped more than 100 points in the past five years. The faculty is better, too, and much better paid than a few years ago.[15]

The Cass and Birnbaum 1965 Edition of *Comparative Guide to American Colleges,* normally silent in praise of changes still going on at a college, noted:

Knox's student body is above average in academic capability; it is the result of systematic efforts in recent years to raise scholastic standards. Administration is seeking to build a first-rate liberal arts college and appears to be making some progress.[16]

New flexibility and content were introduced into the curriculum, opportunities for independent study were increased, and new buildings were constructed, including a fine arts building, dormitories, and a student union. This was tangible, exciting evidence of change, much of it occurring as had been projected in the earlier plan.

Some changes did not occur as originally planned, however; the differences between the Tickton plan and what actually had occurred four years later are instructive. The academic quality of the entering classes, as measured by aptitude test scores and by secondary school rank-in-class had indeed increased substantially. The number of students enrolled also increased, but not as much as the original targets called for: an enrollment of 1250 had been projected for 1963–64, but the actual enrollment that year was 1092, or some 13 percent less. This was true even though the tuition increases originally planned had been modified; the 1959 projection assumed a tuition rate of $1525 during 1963–64, but the actual charge that year was $1465. As a combined result, Knox College received in tuition income that year a total of $1,600,000, or more than $300,000 less than the $1,905,661 envisioned by the 1959 projection. For the total 1963–64 operating budget projected in the original plan, this shortfall of tuition income represented about 8 percent of the total income projected.

Meanwhile, the 1959 projections also suggested an increase in the proportion of students receiving scholarship assistance at Knox from 47 percent in 1959 to 52 percent in 1963–64; the actual percentage in 1963–64 was about 58 percent. About 350 students instead of the projected 200 were receiving loan assistance that year. The sharply increased demands for financial aid—occurring because most of Knox's enrollment increase was an increase in needy students—would have had severe consequences for the overall financial health of the college if the years between 1959 and 1963 had not also been the years when substantial student financial aid was beginning to be supplied from government sources. The Illinois State Scholarship Program, started in 1958–59, was by 1963–64 providing about a quarter of all the scholarship money received by Knox students. Student loans under the National Defense Education Act of 1958 were, by 1963–64, providing three quarters of the loan amount received by Knox students that year. These two outside sources in 1963–64 provided $334,710 in financial aid to Knox students.[17]

Crucial assumptions

One of the critical assumptions about Knox's external environment underlying the 1959 projections (though not explicitly stated there) was that the college was operating primarily in a statewide market where student families' ability and willingness to meet sharply rising tuition costs would not interfere with fulfilling the joint goals of higher student SAT scores, larger enrollment, and increased income (to pay for improved programs) achieved mainly by increased charges to students. The increase in student aid originally projected, as discussed above, was relatively mild, all things considered. The proportion of Knox students coming from out-of-state was to rise (according to the 1959 projections) from 20 percent in 1959–60 to only 24 percent in 1963–64, where it was to stabilize through 1967–68.

As late as the spring of 1963, Tickton seemed to believe that the pool of bright and prosperous college candidates still was large enough to give colleges like Knox adequate leeway for further and sharp tuition increases. While discussing the Ashford College case at a seminar in Cambridge, Massachusetts sponsored by the Ford Foundation, Tickton said:

> The future financing of the operating costs of most private colleges lies mainly in appealing to willing students, rather than to reluctant donors. The students will be there; they can afford to go to college; and many will be willing to pay a good price for the high-quality education that many colleges can provide. The future of private colleges depends, it seems to me, upon their ability to do the job required.[18]

Three other attempts to appraise and understand what happened at Knox follow. They suggest more complex, less optimistic conclusions. The most cogent and most comprehensive explanation is provided by Walter M. North, Director of Student Assistance at Knox. The second explanation, also known to the Knox administration during this period, is offered in terms of a rising trend in the cost to students of attending Knox College, compared with less-rapidly rising costs at other nearby colleges, as shown in Table II-1. A third explanation, which furthers understanding of the difficulties Knox faced and increases respect for the results it achieved, can come from examining the rate at which Knox's potential candidate pools were shrinking as Knox re-defined them over the years by expecting higher academic qualifications and higher student tuition payments; this is the approach defined at the beginning of Chapter II.

Knox official appraises results

Walter North's explanation of what happened at Knox, written in 1964, is part of Knox's continuing, overall effort to appraise its experience and adjust its plans accordingly. (Remember in reading this explanation that Knox during this period was admitting over 80 percent of those applying; major changes in the size, background, or quality of the enrolled student body, therefore, required not only changes in selection policy, but more important, changes in who applied in the first place.)

All of the material presented leads to the same conclusions. In the early 'fifties a policy decision was made to move towards placing a price on education at Knox more equal to the actual cost of providing that education. After income from other sources, the remainder of the cost has been translated into student fees. We have been successful in placing a more realistic price on our product and our services.

The policy proposed that we would not only price realistically but in doing so we would transfer a larger share of the cost to the student.

College policy in other respects has never permitted us to achieve the latter intent. To do so would have required assistance budgets to hold fairly constant while fees went up. For good reason it has not been practical to use ability-to-pay as the determining admission standard. The necessity of a student body of desired size and quality

TABLE II-1

Total costs to Illinois students (including allowance for personal expenses but not for travel) for a resident year at selected midwestern colleges, 1958–59 and 1965–66, ranked by order of cost in 1958–59 *

Institution	Resident student budget 1958–59	Rank order by cost 1958–59	Resident student budget 1965–66	Rank order by cost 1965–66	Percent increase in cost between 1958–59 and 1965–66
Northwestern University	$2400	1	$3270	1	+36%
University of Chicago	2029	2	3250	2	+60%
KNOX COLLEGE	1885	3	3100	3	+64%
Lake Forest College	1850	4	3000	4	+62%
University of Michigan (out-of-state)	1840	5	2250	6	+22%
Monmouth College	1705	6	2800	5	+64%
University of Illinois (in-state)	1450	7	1580	7	+9%

* Information provided by Earl R. Fielder, College Scholarship Service, Educational Testing Service, Princeton, N.J., from student budgets submitted by colleges for use in estimating financial need. This list is illustrative only and does not include several of the public and private colleges which many of the Knox potential and actual candidates were choosing among. Lake Forest College, like Knox, had gone through a self-study and had built a Tickton Method long-range plan, and, also like Knox, had subsequently received a two million dollar development grant from the Ford Foundation to help realize its plans.

and a commitment to find some way for the deserving and promising student to attend regardless of resources have combined to frustrate the economic goal of the policy stated. As we have increased our fees we have created additional need and have increased assistance to meet the need. The increased fees have represented not only an increase in costs to the students but to the collge in the form of assistance. . . . In writing a better price tag we succeeded in increasing the dollar cost to the students while the proportion of the total cost borne by the students has decreased.

.   .   .

As we sought to increase our size and raise our fees, we do not seem to have anticipated correctly the number of students who could successfully finance an education at Knox and at the same time meet the admissions requirements we were imposing. An extension of this would seem to be the fact that until recently we failed to extend our recruitment area in the manner which was required in the face of other factors.[19]

Knox student budget trend compared with competitors'

What can be said of Knox's successive student budgets compared with those of the immediate competition? The relationship between what a year at Knox College cost and what the nation's families could pay was only slightly more restricted (for Knox) in 1963–64 than in 1958–59.[20] However, Knox charges to students did move up noticeably faster than did those of the college's immediate competition. Since Knox was changing the quality and kind of instruction offered, there was internal-cost justification for this move, but until news of the changes were fully communicated to the prospective applicant group, the recruitment task was expected to be increasingly difficult. Table II-1, on the preceding page, illustrates the kind of relative change that was taking place between Knox pricing and that of some of the competition.

At first glance, looking only at the rank-ordering of colleges in the table, it appears that most colleges, including Knox, stayed in line; that is, they tended to maintain their relative position with respect to the total expenses they required of students.

However, it is also true that the percentage increase in Knox's total student cost was the highest of any in this particular group; by 1963–64 the difference in cost between attending Knox for a year and attending Northwestern—the most expensive college in the list—had decreased from $515 to $170. The cost difference between Knox and the Univesity of Michigan (out-of-state student budget) had widened from $45 to $850, and that between Knox and the University of Illinois (in-state student budget) had widened from $435 to $1520.

These are changes substantial enough so that anyone experienced in admissions would probably expect them to set up significant competitive pressures which were unfavorable to Knox's attempts to enroll more full-paying students. (The cost differences would be less, or perhaps even favorable to Knox, for students considering attending Knox *with* financial aid versus attending a public, or private college *without* it.) Just how much extra money families were willing to pay to send a son or daughter to Knox cannot be known, however, without a sophisticated and detailed knowledge of how attracted they were by the opportunities of all kinds which they saw in the colleges available to them. This information is not available. It goes well beyond the still important matters of student budgets and ability to pay. Because the more detailed analysis cannot be made here, no attempt will be made to suggest exactly how important the cost trends shown above actually were to Knox's experience—other than to suggest that the trends seemed important to Knox at the time, and important in retrospect.

Changes in the Knox candidate pool

Finally, it is also possible to examine the approximate shrinkage that occurred in the size of the prospective full-paying candidate pool for Knox College, defined both by minimum SAT scores and by family income.

If one defines a verbal SAT score of 420 as the effective minimum for entering Knox College students in 1959–60, and $1550 as the family contribution necessary to support a student there without further financial aid that year, one can estimate that the number of male and female high school graduates in the nation able to meet or exceed these conditions was about 175,000 students. By 1963–64 the effective minimum SAT verbal score had become about 464, and the family contribution for a student without financial aid had become about $2400; under these new conditions, the national candidate pool for Knox had shrunk to about 151,000 students. Furthermore, if one assumes that the distribution of family income and measured ability is about the same for high school graduates in Illinois as for the whole nation (it is probably slightly higher on both counts) one may also estimate that the Illinois candidate pools thus defined decreased from about 7700 to about 6400 students between 1959–60 and 1963–64. When one considers the shrinkage in candidate pools, as Knox was effectively defining them, and the increasing expense of attending Knox compared with some of its major competitors, it seems hardly surprising that the college was unable to increase, within a slowly expanding recruiting area, the number of full-paying students able to meet its rising standards both of measured aptitude and of ability to pay. The surprise is, rather, that Knox was able to hold its own as well as it did.

The example provided earlier, of the University of Puget Sound, illustrated the usefulness of estimating the size of a college's potential applicant pool as a helpful gauge for the recruitment pressures on a college if it plans to change measured aptitude requirements in admissions and/or the level of student budgets.

The Knox College example illustrates in more detail how intimately these questions of student recruitment, tuition policy, and financial aid policy are related to the overall financial health of an institution, and hence to its ability to grow and to improve its quality of instruction. The Knox College example also serves as a reminder that institutional financial planning, through the assumptions which form the base of any budget projection, is closely related to the institution's external environment: to the ability and willingness of students and their families to pay for college education and to changes taking place at competing institutions.

FISK UNIVERSITY AND THE NEGRO MARKET FOR COLLEGE EDUCATION

The case of Fisk University in Nashville, Tennessee will show how the joint distribution of measured aptitude and family income, applied to the Negro high school graduate population, can help one to understand more about the urgent problems confronting predominantly Negro colleges. With survey data just beginning to be available about the family incomes of Negro high school students and about their measured academic aptitude, it is now possible, for the first time, to attempt in these joint terms a rough description of the Negro market for college education in the same way the total market was described earlier in this chapter. Table II-2, on pages 48–49, distributes the highest-testing half of the male Negro high school graduates in 1964–65 this way, while Appendix D describes the data and methods used to construct the table.[21]

The distribution shows, as one might expect, that the family incomes are much lower for Negro high school students than for all U.S. families. It also shows the mean verbal aptitude for these Negro students, converted to the SAT score scale, to be more than 100 points lower than for the total high school graduate population. The combined effect is to produce extremely small pools of candidates for the most academically selective colleges in the country, even if ability to pay is not at issue. More significant for the immediate future of predominantly Negro colleges, the number of Negro high school graduates able to score in the middle range of measured aptitude (let alone the high range) *and* able to pay a major portion of the costs at these colleges is smaller than one might have anticipated. If predominantly white institutions in the north, midwest, and west continue, as they probably will, to draw larger delegations of the brightest and most prosperous Negro students, the opportunity for Negro colleges to raise academic standards, remain solvent, and at the same time remain predominantly Negro seems more limited than one might otherwise have anticipated.

For example, one noticeable new segment of student recruitment competition comes from the Ivy League colleges, where it

TABLE

Joint distribution of U.S. male Negro high school graduates,* 1964–

		Mean, U.S. male Negro high school graduates	
SAT score		248	300
SAT percentile		50	67
Family income (1965)			
Percentile	Amount (possible contribution)		
0	$000	60,500	40,000
	($000)	60,500	40,000
20	$1400	53,800	36,500
	($000)	58,000	39,000
40	$3100	43,900	31,200
	($110)	50,600	35,900
60	$4900	31,900	23,100
	($310)	38,600	29,400
80	$7270	17,600	13,300
	($660)	21,700	18,200
95	$11,300	5000	4000
	($1570)	5900	5600

II-2

distributed by measured verbal aptitude and family income, 65 †

Mean score level for all U.S. male high school graduates 361 84	400 91	450 96	500 98.8	550 99.7
19,500	10,900	4300	1500	400
19,500	10,900	4300	1500	400
18,300	10,400	4200	1500	400
19,400	10,900	4300	1500	400
15,900	9300	3900	1400	400
18,600	10,700	4300	1500	400
12,600	7600	3300	1200	400
16,600	9900	4200	1500	400
7800	4900	2300	900	200
11,800	7700	3600	1300	400
2600	1800	900	400	100
4400	3400	1900	1000	300

* Total: 121,000 (estimated).

† See Appendix A, page 125, for a guide to reading this table.

is reasonable to guess that the enrollment of Negro students has increased more than fivefold—perhaps almost twice that—the past decade. In 1966 these colleges enrolled about 260 male Negro freshmen; one could estimate at least three-quarters of them (195 freshmen) scored 500 or better on the verbal section of the Scholastic Aptitude Test. These 195 students, if the figures in the preceding table are reasonable ones, comprised roughly 13 percent of the male Negro high school graduates in the nation that year who could be expected to score this well. It is further reasonable to guess that the number of male Negro students who can score this well and who enroll in the Ivy League institutions now has become larger than the number who enroll in the predominantly Negro colleges—all this without mentioning similar, growing delegations in private institutions like Stanford, the University of Chicago, and New York University, or in several of the major state universities.[22]

Fisk University is one of the most distinguished of the nation's predominantly Negro colleges. It is an accredited, private liberal arts college enrolling about 1070 men and women. Fisk's former president, Stephen J. Wright, described the situation of able southern Negro students and of his institution in May, 1963 to a Colloquium of the College Scholarship Service at Excelsior Springs, Missouri:

> The gifted Negro student in the South is excluded, for all practical purposes, from the private institutions in this region that have large scholarship funds. Moreover, the institutions that do not, by policy or practice, deny admission to the Negro student do not, on the other hand, seek him out. . . .
>
> Without generous financial aid, only an infinitesimally small number of Negro students will be able, in the immediate future, to attend the best private colleges, wherever they may be located, since such institutions almost invariably charge the highest tuitions. . . .
>
> Institutions like Fisk University will carry, at least for the next decade, the major responsibility for recruiting the gifted Negro students in the Southern region and for providing the major financial aid for them.[23] To the extent that such institutions are successful they will be serving a useful, national purpose.

The financial problems faced by Fisk in attempting to fulfill this sense of mission are severe. Wright continued:

As a private institution, Fisk is forced to charge a relatively high tuition ($798 in 1964–65) in order to maintain an expenditure-per-student for educational purposes that is commensurate, or nearly commensurate, with other good liberal arts colleges. . . . On the other hand, as an institution serving a predominantly Negro enrollment, Fisk University is confronted with several conflicting problems.

The average income of Negro families is only 54 percent of the average of all American families, making high tuition charges very difficult to introduce and to sustain.

Off-campus work opportunities for Negro students in our region are not only limited in number, but also in kind—mainly low paying jobs.

For economic and other reasons, in proportion to their numbers, only one-third as many Negro students are enrolled in colleges and universities as Americans generally. Thus, even modest increases in fees may well retard major increases in the relative numbers of Negroes attending colleges and universities.

As a private liberal arts college, Fisk University seeks to limit its enrollment to the unusually able and promising students. It cooperates, for example, with other member colleges of the United Negro College Fund in the testing of more than 11,000 students annually in the search for able and talented youths. In addition the university conducts a vigorous recruitment program of its own. . . .

In preparing our 10-year budget, we have planned to double tuition by the academic year 1971–72 in order to remain competitive nationally with respect to faculty salaries. Despite this projected increase in tuition, however, the university expects to continue its policy of recruiting able students, whether or not they are able to pay their way fully. This will mean a significant increase in financial aid, especially through scholarships and loans. . . .[24]

During the last six years, tuition at Fisk Universty, as at many other institutions, has nearly doubled, while income for scholarships and on-campus work opportunities have remained substantially the same. During the same period, the amount budgeted for scholarships has more than doubled. This means, of course, that the major source of "income" for the increases in scholarship funds has been remitted tuition. The remission-of-tuition approach to the problem of providing scholarships draws upon funds that might otherwise be used for teachers' salaries and other direct educational expenditures. The extent to which this remission approach may be extended and continued is highly questionable, in view of the apparent and equally urgent need to double faculty salaries by 1971–72.[25]

Although the median SAT score of Fisk's entering class in 1964—a verbal score of 409—was the highest median score reported for any predominantly Negro college in the 1965 edition of Cass and Birnbaum's *Comparative Guide to American Colleges,* the margin by which Fisk hoped to achieve its admission goals seems tight indeed. Fisk reported that in 1964 it admitted about 96 percent of those applying, and that its entering class included only 19 percent of its freshmen who scored 500 and above on the Scholastic Aptitude Test and 6 percent above 600. Approximately 60 percent of the men in a typical entering class do not graduate; about 9 percent of the men fail to graduate for academic reasons.[26]

Meanwhile, less than half of Fisk's students receive scholarships and/or loans. The university in 1965 needed to fill the most prosperous half (or more) of its entering classes from a candidate pool which may be defined quite roughly by a minimum verbal SAT score of about 300 and family incomes of about $9800 (able to contribute $1200 for a son's or daughter's education, according to the College Scholarship Service estimates, the students themselves providing roughly $350 from job earnings to meet the $1550 student budget). Using the joint distribution table above, one may estimate that this pool numbered between 7400 and 13,600 men and a slightly larger number of women.

The problems of active admission recruitment within this group of Negro students seems more difficult than the problem faced by a racially mixed or predominantly white college, in large part because the pool of Negro candidates defined this way is so much smaller, and consequently may be spread more thinly across the country. Furthermore, the increased enrollment of Negro students in colleges outside of the South seems to signal, for the predominantly Negro colleges, severely increased competition in attracting the ablest and most prosperous Negro students.

If these pressures represent what they seem to, a planner at a college like Fisk would seem to have a number of choices as he looks at Table II-2 above and then at his own admissions statistics. As he senses increased difficulty enrolling the highest-aptitude and most prosperous Negro students, he can attempt one or a number of the following:

1. Increase directly competitive confrontation with the institutions that have newly provided this competition.
2. Move his efforts upward on the table—into the relatively small group of high-aptitude but lower-income students. This effort is not a new kind of attempt, however, and it is questionable how much more this, alone, could be expected to accomplish in off-setting the college's new problem in recruitment.
3. Move his efforts towards the left in the table—into the relatively more plentiful group of lower-scoring men and women. This is the easiest move when one considers the external competition, but perhaps more difficult if one considers seriously the institution's historic wish to remain at the leading edge of the Negro community's higher education.
4. Wait, and hope that increasing population and reduced high school dropout among Negro students will enlarge the candidate pools sufficiently to stay ahead of the twin pressures of rising costs and increased competition.
5. Move off the limiting table entirely: devote a major effort to the enrollment of white students.

None of the choices seem like comfortable ones to the outsider; they seem unexpectedly difficult because the Negro market for college education as defined by the table seems to be an unexpectedly restricted one.[27]

FINANCIAL AID IN HARVARD COLLEGE

In the preceding examples and case histories, which illustrated how colleges might appraise their changing position in the market for college education, attention concentrated upon the supply of full-paying students who seemed both academically qualified and sufficiently prosperous to attend different col-

leges without scholarship assistance. The relatively plentiful
student data available at Harvard College makes it possible to
illustrate how the joint distribution tables may be used to appraise the changing potential supply—at different measured-
aptitude levels—of financially needy students as well as of full-
paying ones. This section will also stand aside briefly from the
main path of the argument and observe some of the dangers of
limiting one's attention only to the easily measured variables of
academic aptitude and family income when considering questions of student recruitment and enrollment.

The changing Harvard student mix versus national trends

If one characterizes the recent student admissions history of
Harvard College in only the joint terms of the distribution tables
used earlier, the following patterns emerge. In 1952, one out of
every ten freshmen presented verbal SAT scores below 474, with
nine out of ten scoring above that level. Within three years, the
tenth percentile score of entering freshmen class had moved up
about 50 points on the SAT scale. During the 1960's this upward movement proceeded irregularly and much more slowly;
by 1964 the tenth percentile verbal SAT score for entering
Harvard freshmen was 556. Roughly the same kind of change
occurred in the median score levels: from 583 (in 1952) to 632
(in 1955) to 664 (in 1964). Information about the family income of Harvard freshmen, not just the scholarship students,
is more scarce. One survey conducted in 1947 (median income:
$8425) and another in 1960 (median income: $14,000) indicate
that Harvard freshmen in each of those years represented roughly
the 87th percentile level of family income (families of high school
graduates) in the United States.

Table II-3 compares these survey results for Harvard College
with information for freshmen entering other groups of colleges
provided in 1965 by the American Council on Education data
bank. Neither set of figures have been adjusted; they hence are
not fully comparable since they were gathered in different years.
However, the national percentile levels represented are roughly

TABLE II-3

Estimated median family incomes represented in the Harvard College Classes of 1951 and 1964 (entering in 1947 and 1960) and in selected groups of college freshmen in 1965,* compared with family incomes (families of U.S. high school graduates)

Year	College or group of colleges	Median family income represented in entering class	Percentile level these medians represent among U.S. family incomes (families of U.S. high school graduates) in these years
1947	Harvard	$ 8425	87
1960	Harvard	14,000	87
1965	Select private colleges	13,750	81
1965	Other private colleges	10,500	68
1965	Select public colleges	11,000	70
1965	Other public colleges	8500	58

* American Council on Education categories of colleges.   The individual institutions sampled within each category are the following.

Select private colleges: Tulane University, Reed College, Lebanon Valley College, Iowa Wesleyan College, Union College, Wittenberg College, Fisk University, Occidental College, St. Louis University, Lake Forest College, Oberlin College, Bowdoin College, Vanderbilt University, Williams College, Washington and Lee University, California Institute of Technology, Wellesley College, Northwestern University, Johns Hopkins University, and Mills College.

Other private colleges: Rider College, St. Mary's College (Md.), Our Lady of the Lake College, Wofford College, Johnson C. Smith University, McPherson College, William Jewell College, Gonzaga University, Kentucky Wesleyan College, Emory and Henry College, Marietta College, Guilford College, St. Norbert College, Whitman College, College of New Rochelle, Monmouth College, Adrian College, Allegheny College, George Peabody Teachers College, St. Mary's College (Calif.), Carroll College, Seattle University, University of Denver.

Select public colleges: University of Kansas, University of North Carolina, and the University of Iowa.

Other public colleges: State University College at Oswego (N.Y.), Northwest Missouri State College, Virginia Military Institute, Arizona State University, University of Rhode Island, University of New Mexico, Peru State College, and State University College at Cortland (N.Y.).

comparable since they do take into account the increasing prosperity of U.S. families of high school graduates in the postwar years.

The extent to which the families of U.S. high school graduates were able to afford sending a son to Harvard College is illustrated for three of the most recent ten years in Table II-4. The first column shows the total cost to a student for a year in residence at Harvard College, including tuition, medical fee, room, board, plus a realistic—but far from lavish—allowance for personal expenses, and one hundred dollars (about average in 1955) allowance for travel expenses. The second column lists, for U.S. high school graduates, the 20th percentile level of family incomes. One notices that in 1955 the cost of attending Harvard for a year represented 73 percent of the annual income of a family (of a high school graduate) at the 20th percentile level nationally, while in 1964 the cost of attending Harvard for a year had grown to represent about 91 percent of the income of families at the 20th percentile that year.

The third column shows the income level, for a normal-budget, three-child family, estimated by Harvard College financial aid officers to represent the approximate dividing line between family incomes that could finance a son's year at Harvard unaided by scholarship assistance and those which could not. Estimates of the median income of all Harvard freshmen in the three years (Column 4) are about $1000 less than the corresponding "no-need" boundary estimates (Column 3). The fifth column lists, for U.S. high school graduates, the 90th percentile level of family incomes—or incomes at the bottom of the top tenth of this income distribution. Since the most prosperous ten percent of families in the nation have been increasing their incomes at a more rapid rate (52 percent between 1955 and 1964 for the 90th percentile families) than the least prosperous fifth (whose incomes rose only 35 percent during the same period), and since Harvard's financial need estimates require relatively more contribution from family income at higher income levels, the apparent burden of paying for a year at Harvard actually decreased for families at the 90th percentile level of family income.[28] For the median-income family of a high school graduate

TABLE II-4

Comparison of total student costs for a resident year at Harvard College (including $100 travel allowance) with U.S. family incomes (families of high school graduates) at the 20th and 90th percentile levels and with Harvard College estimated median family incomes and Harvard College "no-need" boundary, 1955, 1960 and 1964 *

Year	Harvard College resident student budget (one year)	U.S. family incomes (families of high school gradu-ates); 20th percentile level	Harvard estimated "no-need" income boundary (normal budget, 3 children in family)	Estimated median family in-come for Harvard entering class	U.S. family incomes (families of high school grad-uates); 90th per-centile level
	Column 1	Column 2	Column 3	Column 4	Column 5
1955–56	$2050	$2810 (1955)	$12,250	$11,250	$12,470 (1955)
1960–61	2930	3320 (1960)	15,250	14,000	15,690 (1960)
1964–65	3470	3800 (1964)	16,500	15,500	19,000 (1964)
Percent change 1955–56 to 1964–65	+69	+35	+35	+38	+52

* Income distributions for families of U.S. high school graduates (Columns 2 and 5) are those used in Appendix A, described in Chapter II and in the notes following the Appendix.   Estimates of median family incomes in entering Harvard classes were made by employing the two income surveys (Classes of 1951 and 1964, entering in 1947 and 1960), and assuming that a constant percentage increase took place in the intervening years and continued to 1964–65.

in the United States, however, the expense of a year at Harvard represented about 40 percent of the annual family income in 1955, and about 48 percent in 1964; for these families, the apparent financial burden of a year at Harvard (without financial aid) clearly increased.

Thus, depending on where one stood in the hierarchy of national family income levels between 1955 and 1964, the burden unaided of the cost of a Harvard education either increased (for middle and low-income families) or decreased (for the highest-income families) compared with family ability to pay. This particular kind of appraisal, however, is not the only financial one which is important to parents when they consider the possible expense of their children's college education; an equal (or greater) concern is how the annual costs at Harvard College compare with those at other available colleges, and to what extent financial aid may be available to help offset those costs.

The major costs of a resident year in Harvard College, as at many private colleges, increased considerably faster in the 1955–64 decade than the comparable costs did for a resident

TABLE II-5

Index of change in cost of tuition and fees, room, and board, at 46 northeastern colleges, 1955–56 to 1963–64 (1955–56 = 100) *

	1955–56	1963–64	Percent increase 1955–56 to 1963–64
Public colleges (5)			
Charges to in-state students	$ 928	$1220	+131
Charges to out-of-state students	1175	1691	+144
Private colleges (41)	1513	2317	+153
Harvard College	1623.50	2615	+161
Family disposable income (after taxes, and including unrelated individuals)			+132

* Information provided by Dr. Allan M. Cartter, Vice-President, American Council on Education.

year at a tax-supported college—either in or outside the student's home state. An index of change between 1955–56 and 1963–64 in the cost of tuition, room, and board can be calculated from information provided by the Office of Statistical Information and Research of the American Council on Education for 46 northeastern colleges, 41 of them private (see Table II-5).

Indices of change

A word of caution is necessary about the interpretation and use of comparative indices purporting to illustrate the changing burdens of college charges versus national ability to pay. If the two series increase at varying rates, as these have since 1900, one may be able to demonstrate almost any conclusions, depending on one's choice of the "normal" or base year for comparison. The following table compares charges at Harvard College with U.S. per capita disposable personal income in selected years from 1899–1900 to 1963–64.

Per capita disposable personal income in the United States increased more rapidly than Harvard charges to students between 1900 and 1928, then declined sharply during the depression while Harvard's charges were reduced only slightly, then rebounded sharply into the postwar period. When one compares the percentage change for each series in selected periods, one can notice the following relationships:

1. Between 1900 and 1964, U.S. per capita disposable personal income increased more than twice as fast as Harvard's total charges to students.
2. Between 1928 and 1964, however, the rate of increase was about the same in both series.
3. Between 1932 and 1964, U.S. per capita disposable personal income increased again more than twice as fast as Harvard's total charges to students.
4. Between 1956 and 1964, Harvard's total charges to students increased twice as fast as U.S. per capita disposable personal income —almost exactly the reverse of 1 and 3 above.

If series like these are used to add objective evidence to a discussion of whether Harvard College charges are rising dan-

TABLE II-6

Harvard College charges to students and U.S. per capita disposable
personal income in selected years 1899–1900 to 1963–64

Year	Harvard College charges to students *			U.S. per capita disposable personal income (current dollars) †
	Tuition and fees	Room and board	Total charges	
1899–1900	$ 150	$ 275	$ 425	$ 185
1927–28	310	460	770	673
1931–32	410	538	948	390
1935–36	410	538	948	518
1939–40	420	504	924	573
1943–44	420	504	924	1057
1947–48	430	591	1021	1290
1951–52	630	675	1305	1518
1955–56	837.50	786	1623.50	1743
1959–60	1318	1035	2353	1937
1963–64	1520	1095	2615	2266
Percent change, selected periods				
1900–64	+914	+299	+515	+1125
1928–64	+390	+138	+240	+ 237
1932–64	+271	+104	+176	+ 481
1956–64	+ 81	+ 39	+ 61	+ 30

* Harvard College tuition, room, board charges supplied by the Harvard
University Comptroller's Office.

† U.S. per capita disposable personal income figures were taken from U.S.
Bureau of the Census, *Historical Statistics of the United States, Colonial
Times to 1957* (Washington, D.C.: U.S. Government Printing Office, 1960),
and from *Economic Report of the President, January 1966* (Washington,
D.C.: U.S. Government Printing Office, 1966), Table C-15, p. 227.

gerously rapidly compared with national ability to pay—or that
they are rising at an unconscionably slow pace—one must remember that the objective evidence must incorporate, first, a
subjective judgment as to the appropriate base year(s) which
will be used for the comparisons.

As was suggested in the Knox College example, the financial
advantage or disadvantage to low- and middle-income students

of attending Harvard compared with most public colleges varies in ways determined by two different pricing systems, private and public. Harvard and many similar private colleges tailor scholarship size to apparent financial need. Most public universities, although there are an increasing number of exceptions, award few scholarships since they have already given each student the benefit of low tuition. Thus a low-income family, if the son receives a Harvard scholarship, may encounter less out-of-pocket cost if the son attends Harvard with a scholarship than if he goes to the state university without one. But at some middle-income level this advantage shifts. The Harvard scholarship for a middle-income family is smaller than it was for the low-income family (the middle-income family is presumed to need less help in meeting the Harvard College costs), and so the total bill at the state university becomes less than the net expense at Harvard.

Scholarship students

During the decade from 1956 to 1966, the median family income for holders of scholarships administered by Harvard College rose from $6000 to $9200, in each case representing roughly the 57th percentile level of family income (families of high school graduates) in the United States. In 1956, roughly a quarter of the student body held these scholarships (other students held awards from outside sources, such as National Merit and General Motors, the two largest ones); by 1966, roughly a third of the students held Harvard-administered scholarships. To maintain this support (and this implied socioeconomic stability) during a period of rapidly rising student budgets, the administration and funding of student financial aid in Harvard College, as in many other private colleges, had to undergo a quiet revolution. The total student financial aid administered by Harvard more than doubled; the amount received by students from outside sources did the same. Between 1954 and 1966, more than 17 million dollars was added to scholarship endowment funds, a larger amount for this purpose than had been received in the college's prior history. Alumni current gifts for scholarships almost doubled. Yet these massive transfusions alone fell significantly short of the expanding needs. Sharply increased student borrowing (made possible by the expansion of Harvard's loan funds and by the National Defense Student Loan Program) and student employment during the academic year were also necessary. By 1964 roughly 40 percent of the student body was borrowing to help meet college expenses, and 40 percent (including considerable overlap with the loan holders) were working an average of 12 hours a week during the academic year at jobs ranging from dining hall work to cleaning dormitories to assisting faculty in their research to operating student-run businesses on a profit-sharing basis.

With this background in mind, what does the kind of analysis suggested at the beginning of this chapter and in Appendix A tell about Harvard's changing position in the national market for college education? What can one say of Harvard College's changing ability to draw the active interest of students from low- and middle-income levels as well as from higher levels and from various selected groups defined by measured aptitude?

Table II-7, which follows, is designed to show how one may begin to subdivide a college's applicant group and appraise change within its different family-income portions and different aptitude-level portions. The table also illustrates how a college with more qualified applicants than space can begin to guess at what its potential impact on the national market might be if it exercised selection policy in different ways—as well as to guess at its actual impact by rough current measurements.

The left-hand portion of the table arbitrarily defines the Harvard College freshman class segments (classes entering in 1955 and 1964) and the comparably defined national pools of interest. In both years, a verbal SAT score of 520 roughly defines a score level which the great majority of the entering Harvard students could have equaled or bettered. In 1955, a "normal-budget" family with three children, receiving $12,500 income annually, was estimated to represent the approximate borderline level of income which separated families whose sons needed scholarship assistance at Harvard and families which did not. For 1964, because of the growing cost of attending Harvard, this borderline income level had increased, as estimated by Harvard's financial aid officers, to about $16,500. It is a rare family which is "normal" in its annual budget; most families either benefit from extra assets, or carry extra burdens, or both. Therefore, the "no-need" borderline for Harvard College in practice varied from family to family depending upon individual circumstances.

The first column in the table lists the total number of applicants which meet the various joint income and aptitude specifications. Since most of these applicants applied to other colleges as well as Harvard, and since not all of those admitted would have chosen to enroll, the second column deflates the total applicant numbers in Column One to approximate the number who might actually have enrolled if admitted. In 1955, 61 percent of those admitted actually enrolled; in 1964, 83 percent did. In Column Three, national pools of male high school graduates, comparably defined as to income and aptitude, come from the "best-guess" set of estimates in Appendix A. Column Five distributes Harvard freshman registrants in the same manner as the applicants were distributed in the first two columns. Percent-of-market or "market impact" calculations are shown in Columns Four and Six.

Harvard's impact on the national market

With the information presented in this way, the table yields a number of findings one might have expected, and one or two surprises. It is hardly surprising, when one compares in Column Six the similarly defined segments for 1955 and 1964, that the actual impact of Harvard College freshman registrations upon the national pools has in each instance declined. Harvard freshman classes expanded only slightly while the national pools roughly doubled in size. One element, a correct one, of Harvard College's reputation is that it is an expensive place to study. In the face of rising student expenses, it is perhaps mildly surprising to see that both among "effective" applicants (Column Four) and registrants (Column Six), Harvard's national-market impact in the low income segments of the table (Lines 2 and 5) in-

TABLE II-7

Relationship of selected groups of Harvard applicants and registrants in the Classes of 1959 and 1968 (entering in 1955 and 1964)—groups defined by SAT verbal score *and* family income—to the correspondingly defined pools of U.S. male high school graduates,* 1955 and 1964

Harvard College class segment definitions	Total number of applicants in each Harvard class segment	Number of "effective" applicants in each segment after allowing for men who would not enroll if admitted	Number of U.S. male high school graduates, same year, defined by same SAT *and* income conditions	Harvard "effective" applicants (Column 2) as a percentage of comparable national market segment (Column 3)	Number of registrants in each Harvard class segment	Harvard registrants (Column 5) as a percentage of comparable national market segment (Column 3)
	Column 1	Column 2	Column 3	Column 4	Column 5	Column 6
Class of 1959						
1. V520 or higher; all income levels	3452	2106	59,000	3.6	1010	1.7
2. V520 or higher; family income less than $12,250	1765	1077	42,000	2.6	508	1.2
3. V520 or higher; family income $12,250 or more	1687	1029	17,000	6.0	502	2.9
4. V650 or higher; all income levels	1565	955	5000	19.1	458	9.1
5. V650 or higher; family income less than $12,250	797	487	3000	16.2	226	7.5
6. V650 or higher; family income $12,250 or more	768	468	2000	23.4	232	11.6
Class of 1968						
1. V520 or higher; all income levels	5022	4168	109,000	3.8	1141	1.0
2. V520 or higher; family income less than $16,500	2795	2320	73,000	3.2	611	0.8

3. V520 or higher; family income $16,500 or more	2227	1848	36,000	530	5.1	1.5
4. V650 or higher; all income levels	2652	2201	9000	661	24.5	7.3
5. V650 or higher; family income less than $16,500	1476	1225	4000	354	30.6	8.9
6. V650 or higher; family income $16,500 or more	1176	976	5000	307	19.5	6.1

Total admission and financial aid summary statistics of application and registration for the Classes of 1959 and 1968

	Class of 1959		Class of 1968	
	Applicants	Registrants	Applicants	Registrants
Number of Candidates for Admission and Financial Aid:	1942		3141	
Number enrolled with Harvard scholarship		316		411
Number enrolled but denied Harvard scholarship (many received awards from sources outside Harvard)		235		232
Number of Candidates for Admission only:	1874	565	2502	558
Totals	3816	1116	5643	1201

* The total number of U.S. male high school graduates in 1954–55 was 648,000 and in 1963–64 was 1,129,000.

creased more rapidly (or declined more slowly) than its impact in the high-income segments (Lines 3 and 6). Undoubtedly the unusual strength of the College financial aid program helped, as did special efforts by alumni Schools and Scholarship committees and admission staff members to maintain broad contact with all kinds of school districts, and not merely the prosperous ones. Many colleges, however, were making similar attempts; Harvard's effort was not unique. Perhaps the most surprising feature of the table is the unexpectedly large potential impact and actual impact Harvard had upon the high-measured-aptitude segment of the national market. "Potential impact" here can be defined as the impact Harvard would have had if it had admitted all who applied in each segment, and then enrolled all those from the admitted group who wished to attend. Both the potential (Column Four) and actual (Column Six) impact is far greater in the high-score segment than in the lower-score one; in 1964, for example, Harvard apparently had both the drawing power and the space to make up four-fifths of its entering class with men who could both score above 650 on the SAT and also meet without scholarship aid the annual costs of attending. This represented nearly a fifth of the male candidates of this description in the nation. (Its potential drawing power seemed even stronger among the similar-aptitude but lower-income group which would need scholarship assistance to attend.) This theoretically possible shift in selection practice is an extreme illustration, not one likely to occur by decision of the present faculty Committee on Admissions and Scholarships, even though Harvard's potential drawing power in this particular segment of the market seems to be without equal at any other college in the United States. But a significant number of institutions have it in their power, whether by drift or design, to make a noticeable aggregate impact. If many of these colleges moved their policy only a moderate distance in this direction the effect could indeed be great—as it has been already during the past ten years. Since the potential impact is considerably greater than one might otherwise have guessed, the issues of admission and financial aid policy in those colleges may be also of greater general interest regardless of one's view as to what the outcome should be.

Aggregate statistics versus individual performance

Having dealt with the possible help a variety of individual private colleges might gain from using the joint aptitude-and-family-income analysis to examine their own situations, it also seems worthwhile to illustrate some of the pitfalls which seem inherent in placing undue emphasis on these two variables alone. It is easy, for example, to begin to think of scores on a measured aptitude scale as a kind of clean shorthand for describing both present intellectual alertness and future academic promise. If in individual cases all other things were equal—past habits of performance, attitude, health, and stamina, merely beginning the list of important elements which never are equal—then the SAT shorthand might be able to carry this predictive burden tolerably well.[29] As it is, SAT scores (or these taken in combination with some index of performance in high school) remain imperfect to operate even an admissions policy which might seek optimum academic performance as its only goal. The Harvard College Class of 1968, for example, first enrolled in the fall of 1964 with a median verbal SAT score of 664, 29 points lower than the median for the preceding class and 13 points lower than for the one before that. The generally prevailing opinion of teachers, deans, and housemasters has been that the Class of 1968 is one of the most active and interesting classes in recent years, considerably more so than either the Class of 1967 or the Class of 1966. The academic performance of the Class of 1968, measured by percentage of students receiving honor grades, was better at the end of its freshman year than for any prior Harvard class in recent history.[30]

If one examines the verbal SAT score distribution of the scholars who, upon graduation from college, received the highest academic honors in the Class of 1962, one finds that about a quarter of the summa cum laude graduates and about a third of the magna cum laude graduates would not have been admitted in the first place if the verbal SAT score median for that class (659) had instead been the minimum score. The following Table II-8 illustrates this distribution.

While no device has yet been invented which can be used

TABLE II-8

Number and percentage of high honor graduates in the Harvard College Class of 1962 who scored above and below the class median (659) on the verbal section of the Scholastic Aptitude Test in high school

	Graduation Honors					
	Summa cum laude		Magna cum laude with highest honors		Magna cum laude	
SAT verbal score range at entrance	Number	(percentage)	Number	(percentage)	Number	(percentage)
659 and above	14	(73.7)	5	(62.5)	133	(66.8)
658 and below	5	(26.3)	3	(37.5)	60	(33.2)

as a precise measure of genuinely creative work done in college, let alone any agreement as to just how "creative" should be defined, one approximate indication in Harvard College, is the annual awarding of the David McCord Prizes. The winners are selected from nominations submitted by the housemasters for undergraduates "who have demonstrated unusual creative ability and stamina in writing, or in music, painting, drawing or sculpture." [31]   Among the thirty undergraduate winners during the first four years in which the prizes were awarded (1960 through 1963) half of them presented verbal aptitude scores at admission in the 659-and-above range, and half below this level.

One cannot say that the record of high honors or of creative distinction achieved by these men is better (or worse) than that which might have been compiled by replacements selected on the basis of higher SAT scores. It is possible that it is worse. One can say, however, that some of the men who at entrance scored in the bottom half of their freshman class, ranked by SAT scores, did perform extremely well but would not have been given that opportunity under an admission policy which was much more heavily aptitude-test-oriented.

Measured aptitude versus student diversity

Furthermore, if one characterizes the majority of Harvard's students as urban-suburban, from business or professional families, prosperous by national standards, and relatively sophisticated, and if one would like if possible to preserve or extend the range of socioeconomic diversity represented in successive entering classes (there are other kinds of diversity one might be concerned about), then it should be possible to identify the most-different minority elements and see the extent to which their representation in the class would be affected by, for example, a sharp increase in the effective minimum SAT score.

Three groups in the Class of 1969, which entered in 1965, are chosen below for this kind of rough analysis.

1. Men who, all things considered, seemed to come from disadvantaged cultural and/or economic circumstances. Usually their family incomes were less than $5,000 a year and usually they received poor academic preparation for college. Twenty of the twenty-five men thus classified were Negroes.
2. Men who came from genuinely rural backgrounds, and generally seemed less sophisticated than the majority of their classmates. Thirty-two men were thus classified.
3. Sons of factory or day laborers (and not included in either of the two categories above). Forty-nine men were in this category.

Foreign students, though noticeably different in their educational backgrounds, are not included above because they are not required to take the Scholastic Aptitude Test, and often do not. The 106 men who make up the three groups listed above (8.8 percent of the class) do not include all of the men whom one would regard as low-income in background or bringing socioeconomic diversity to the college.

Table II-9 shows that the men in these three groups tend to cluster at the lower portions of the verbal SAT score distribution for the class as a whole. If, for example, the median SAT score for the class, 679, had instead been the minimum score, 75 of the 106 men in these three groups (70.8 percent of them) would not have been admitted.

TABLE II-9

Number of men in the Class of 1969 in each verbal aptitude score (SAT) decile who could be classified "disadvantaged" or "rural" or were sons of laborers and also not included in the above two groupings. (Figures in parentheses in Column 5 are the percentages those groups represent of each decile in the class. For example, in the tenth decile the three groups accounted for 22 men, or 18.2 percent of the 121 men in the decile.)

SAT deciles in the Class of 1969	Column 1 SAT verbal score range for each decile	Column 2 Disadvantaged	Column 3 Rural	Column 4 Laborer sons (not included elsewhere)	Column 5 Subtotal Columns 2 through 4 (Figures in parenthesis represent the subtotal's percentage of the Column 6 totals.)	Column 6 Total number of men in the Class of 1969 in each SAT decile
1st	755–800	1	0	2	3 (2.5%)	120
2nd	734–754	0	0	5	5 (4.1%)	121
3rd	718–733	1	2	2	5 (4.2%)	120
4th	697–717	2	3	5	10 (8.3%)	121
5th	679–696	1	3	4	8 (6.7%)	120
6th	658–678	2	7	8	17 (14.1%)	121
7th	637–657	4	7	6	17 (14.2%)	120
8th	604–636	3	2	6	11 (9.1%)	121
9th	572–603	4	1	3	8 (6.7%)	120
10th	0–571	7	7	8	22 (18.2%)	121
TOTALS		25	32	49	106	1205

One of the obvious effects of raising of the minimum SAT scores for the entering class to 679, however, would have been financial. While the 106 members of these three groups received some financial aid (an estimated $16,500) from outside sources such as the National Merit Scholarship Program, 83 received Harvard freshman scholarships, which in turn accounted for 20 percent of the total number of Harvard freshman scholarships awarded that year. The 83 awards totaled $141,700, or 24.2 percent of the total freshman scholarship budget (an amount considerably greater than Radcliffe College spends for all of its freshman scholarships). If the minimum verbal SAT score that year had been 679, and if 63 awards from these three groups had not been made because these present scholarship holders scored below 679 (here the ungenerous assumption is made that these men would have been replaced by more prosperous students who could pay their own way), the freshman scholarship expenditure in these three groups alone would have been reduced by $105,100, or a reduction of 17.9 percent in the total expenditure for Harvard freshman scholarships. Since these three groups represent only a partial enumeration of the scholarship holders who scored below 679, the statement of potential savings is incomplete. In fact, however, if the SAT minimum score was raised to 679, it is unlikely that all of the higher-scoring replacements for the present bottom half of the class would be nonscholarship students. Yet because of the correlation already observed between SAT scores and family income, it seems probable that the aggregate student financial need—holding other factors constant in admissions policy—still would be less than it is now.

The example of lower-scoring Harvard freshmen performing surprisingly well academically in comparison with their higher-scoring contemporaries is not included in an attempt to deal with the subject of appropriate criteria for predicting high academic achievement; the enumeration of minority subgroups who would largely be selected out of Harvard College if a high-minimum-SAT selection policy were introduced is not included here in attempt to say what kind of student diversity or homogeneity a college ought to try to achieve, along with its intellectual objectives, in training graduates for productive life in a diverse society. The examples are included, however, to demonstrate explicitly that these issues do exist, that they are important, and that the joint distribution approach, which appraises only measured aptitude and family income, cannot by itself be made to deal effectively with these issues.

GROUPS OF COLLEGES AND THEIR STUDENT MARKETS

Unfortunately, there is no nationwide, periodic census taken to record what changes in admission practice are taking place in groups of similar colleges. It would be helpful, for example, to know for each college the number of students applying, accepted, and enrolled, with the students further classified by measured ability, by expected family financial contribution (this data would be available at least for the scholarship candidates and loan applicants), and perhaps also by state of residence.

The College Entrance Examination Board began in the early 1960's to collect and publish some of this information on a voluntary and limited basis, in its biennial survey, *Manual of Freshman Class Profiles.* This work permits a glimpse of what is happening in the colleges and universities that have reported comparable information.

Consider, then, how the joint distribution tables of Appendix A might be used for appraising changes in the market for higher education for a group of colleges. In Appendix C, student expense budgets and 10th percentile SAT score levels for entering freshmen are listed for 39 colleges, separated into six more or less homogeneous groups.

> Selective private universities (7 colleges)
> Selective private liberal arts colleges (8 colleges)
> Selective eastern women's colleges (6 colleges)
> Small midwest private liberal arts colleges (7 colleges)
> Engineering colleges (6 colleges)
> Public universities (5 colleges)

If one compares average data for the entering freshman classes in 1962 and 1964 in each group of colleges, one notes that the increase in student expense budgets ranged from $115 (selective private universities) to $240 (small midwest private liberal arts colleges, and out-of-state student budgets at the public universities); the increase in 10th percentile level SAT scores increased from 2 points (selective eastern women's colleges) [32] to 30 points (engineering colleges). The period of comparison is too short and the number of colleges reporting comparable data in each group is too small to define properly the longer trends, but the direction and rough magnitudes still are interesting—both for themselves, and for what they show when combined with the tables of Appendix A. As an example, the data in Appendix C for the seven selective private universities is reproduced in Table II-10.

The mean student expense budget (room, board, tuition, personal expenses) for these universities in 1962 was roughly $2845 a year; by 1964 it had increased $115, or 4 percent, to $2960. The 10th percentile level of Scholastic Aptitude Test verbal scores for entering freshmen (the group mean for the 10th percentile level) was 524 in 1962 and 550 in 1964. If one enters the 1962 table in Appendix A for a family contribution of $2045 (figuring most of these colleges expect the student himself to provide roughly $800 more, total expenses thus equalling $2845), and for an SAT score of 524, one can estimate that these universities in 1962 were drawing their nonscholarship students— over half their entering classes—from a potential candidate pool of 34,000 male high school graduates. One can also derive from the tables the effects in 1964 of the budget change alone, the score change alone, and the combined effect of both changes together.

1. Pool size, 1964, assuming $115 increase in student expense budgets, but no change in SAT scores: 43,000.
2. Pool size, 1964, assuming score level increases from 524 to 550, but no change in expense budgets: 30,000.
3. Pool size, 1964, actual, accounting for both changes: 29,000.

TABLE II-10

Change in student expense budgets and minimum effective (10th percentile) Scholastic Aptitude Test verbal score levels for enrolled freshmen in seven selective private universities, 1962–64

	Total student expense for one resident year		Percentage of students receiving financial aid	Scholastic Aptitude Test verbal score for 10th percentile level of enrolled entering class	
	1962	*1964*	*1964*	*1962*	*1964*
Cornell University *	$3025	$3225	33%	555 †	560 †
Dartmouth College	2900	3000	40%	552	572
Duke University	2200	2400	40%	460 †	520 †
University of Pennsylvania	3050	3050	40%	475	500
Princeton University	3060	3080	40%	558	569
Stanford University	2685	2940	35%	522 †	541 †
Yale University	3000	3000	40%	547	585
Mean:	$2845	$2960	Mean:	524	550
Change:		+$115	Change:		+26 points

* College of Arts and Sciences only.
† Scores here are for men only.

The first hypothetical example of change taking place by 1964, with expense budgets increasing moderately, but unchanging score levels, yields the kind of increase in candidate pool size which most of the articles on admissions in the national press have led us to expect. After all, family incomes at the 80th percentile level in the nation increased over 9 percent, while the combined student expense budgets of the seven universities during this period increased only 4 percent. This more rapid rise of family income (compared with student cost increases) serves to expand the effective candidate pool. Furthermore, 1962 through 1964 was the period when the babies born just after World War II began to go to college. The number of male high school graduates in this period increased over 15 percent.[33]

However, the 26-point upward movement of test score levels in 1964 had an even more powerful effect. The net result, taking into account all of the changes, was to *reduce* the size of the effective nonscholarship candidate pool of male high school graduates for these universities by about 14 percent—or 7 percent a year for 1963 and 1964!

The data for the eight selective private liberal arts colleges in Appendix A is similar to that for the universities, and would have been even more so but for the inclusion of Williams College, whose 10th percentile SAT score level dropped 14 points as the college expanded its foundation-supported plan to experiment with the admission and education of special categories of more "high risk" candidates, many of whom presented lower SAT scores for admission than was usual for candidates admitted to Williams in recent years.

The selective eastern women's colleges showed the least upward movement in their test score patterns of any of the groups studied. But then, the most lenient of these six colleges (Vassar) in 1962 was already drawing 90 percent of its freshmen from the top ten percent of the women SAT test-takers in that graduating high school generation, and the most stringent college (Radcliffe) drew 90 percent of its students from the top 2 percent!

Patterns illustrated by the seven small midwestern private liberal arts colleges and the six engineering colleges were similar to those of the selective universities and selective liberal arts colleges, although roughly 100 points lower on the SAT score scale. Similar movement took place in the public university pattern, although the sample available from the *Manual of Freshman Class Profiles* for these institutions is too small for anything but speculative illustration.

For college faculties and administrations seeking to enroll more of the bright and the prosperous, the patterns give clear notice that many other institutions are proceeding in well-intentioned lockstep towards the same destination and that the pathway is getting crowded. For state legislators, the changing patterns add evidence that one major job at hand, if the best-established institutions collectively pursue their present course, is provision of higher education for students of medium aptitude and middle or low family income. For those concerned about maintaining flexibility and the opportunity for mobility within our system of secondary and higher education, the patterns warn that the freshman classes in many colleges are becoming increasingly homogeneous—at least as measured by test scores and by the family incomes of the nonscholarship students.

THE FEDERAL GOVERNMENT AND THE MARKET

If the additional federal resources devoted to student aid are committed primarily to fill the gap between other aid sources and the amount necessary for the whole system of higher education to provide universal (however it comes to be defined) opportunity for higher education, it then becomes important to measure the gap. That measurement will always be complicated by the difficulty of first defining just which gap it is that should be filled. Should higher education be compulsory for everyone? If not, are there limits to what categories of students merit federal support—either limits of measured ability or limits measured by prior performance in secondary school? Questions like these must precede the attempt to define the total needs and goals for higher education. In all probability, short of universal and compulsory higher education, it will be impossible to define any one set of "right" answers to these questions. The answers will change, depending on what the total system of primary and secondary education seems to be producing, on what the labor force seems to demand, and on how much the nation thinks it can afford as the years pass. This said, it still seems desirable for federal legislators and administrators both to be able to cost out different limits and goals for federal student aid, and also to measure in some rough way the effect of past programs.

How much student aid is needed?

One can say readily enough how much it will cost to give 140,000 scholarships averaging $500 each (the first-year authorization for grants to low-income college students under the Higher Education Act of 1965), or how much it will cost to make available a given number of federal loans or work-study jobs of a given average size, but it is much harder now to say how far this moves the nation towards any definition it is likely to make of universal opportunity for higher education. In order to accomplish this last, it seems necessary to have some idea of the following, at the very least.

1. How many candidates for higher education there will probably be in any year, with what rough academic qualifications, and—if one wishes to award direct student aid in some relation to student financial need—with what financial resources already available to them.
2. How these candidates now distribute themselves throughout our present system of higher education.
3. How many realistic candidates (however one decides to define realistic) do not go on to higher education, and for what reasons.
4. How much financial aid of what kind (scholarship, loan, or job) and from what sources goes to which students (classified at least by some academic measurement and some ability-to-pay measurement) in which kinds of institutions.
5. In what specific areas the actual pattern falls furthest short of the desired one, and by how much.
6. How these patterns seem to be changing over time.

Note again that these are the questions one might ask if concerned, as this study is in part, with the problem of more efficiently making supplementary, direct student aid grants available from government sources in order to help a mixed system of higher education become hospitable to more students. If one is primarily concerned with a different problem, such as how to provide a system of direct, general-purpose subsidy from governments to colleges, public and private, or how much it costs to provide a network of institutions different in kind and purpose from the institutions now existing, then one of course asks different questions.

Attempts to find nationwide answers to the questions listed above began seriously in the last two or three years, and these beginnings, measured by the standard of what was known previously, are promising indeed. Measured by the standard of what should be known before we decide to spend half a billion dollars a year or one billion or three billion, our knowledge is surprisingly inadequate.

Meager information

Relatively good total enrollment figures for schools and colleges are maintained now by the U.S. Office of Education, and a good body of research exists about the national talent supply, measured by aptitude tests. But knowledge of how this ability pool distributes itself (or fails to distribute itself) in colleges across the nation is spotty indeed. The *Manuals of Freshman Class Profiles* series is helpful, but reporting is voluntary, incomplete, and concentrated in the relatively prosperous colleges and in the colleges associated with the College Entrance Examination Board. A sample survey conducted by the American Council on Education for the U.S. Office of Education provides more information about other kinds of institutions of higher education and their student populations; the results of this survey, not available at the time of this writing, will undoubtedly profit by cross-checking with others yet to be made.

Still, however, we have relatively little measurement of how these patterns are changing and, most important for the federal and state governments, there is no comprehensive survey completed or in progress which relates what kinds of student aid from what sources are going to which students (grouped by financial need and by academic performance or potential), in which institutions of higher education. Without this basic information about the destination of student aid of all kinds it becomes much harder to estimate sensibly any gap between present effort and needed effort.

This is not to say that good educational policy cannot emerge at the federal and state levels without extensive prior surveys. The acts creating the federal Land Grant College subsidies a hundred years ago and the G.I. Bill twenty years ago did not benefit—or suffer—from much prior or concurrent measurement of this kind. It is to say, however, that with higher education now in the process of rapid change, and likely to create as many new places for students in the next fifteen years as it did in the last three hundred, with other insistent demands increasing upon the federal budget, we seem to be entering a period when colleges will be more likely than they were in more stable enrollment periods to budget wastefully for student aid in higher education: if we fail to budget enough we lose relatively larger increments of trained talent than was likely before, and if we budget too much we draw more heavily than before upon resources which might better be used elsewhere.

A symptom of past failure to maintain adequate statistics is the extremely wide range of policy positions which are advanced seriously when federal aid to college students is discussed. At one extreme are the surveys every spring (often commented upon in the general circulation portions of financial press: Wall Street Journal, Kiplinger letter, and so on) which list colleges with spaces still open for the following year, and with scholarship money still unclaimed. The implication is clear: if college places and college scholarships are going begging, how can we possibly be seriously concerned about rushing to bring about great increases in college capacity and commit new amounts to student aid? In direct opposition stand a number of planning studies which project a great need to expand college capacity and supplementary student aid. For example, in 1964 Rexford G. Moon, Jr., then director of the College Scholarship Service, proposed a model to assess what the national need to provide college student aid (after parents contributed all that could be expected) might be in 1970.[34] Moon estimated that the need for college student aid, after parent and student contributions, would be almost 2 billion dollars a year by 1970, or more than four times what was available in 1960. He proceeded to this conclusion as follows.

1. Project the income distribution of families most likely to be sending sons and daughters to college in 1970.
2. Project enrollment in higher education in 1970, and make sub-estimates of how this enrollment may distribute among part-time (35 percent) and full-time (65 percent) enrollment in two-year colleges, public four-year colleges, and private four-year colleges. (The first two steps require crucial assumptions about college-going patterns we now know uncomfortably little about—as has been discussed earlier in this chapter.)

3. Estimate what the expenses to students will be in these institutions in 1970.
4. Estimate what portion of these expenses might reasonably be met by families of students, and by the students themselves. (This, of course, also depends on the levels of family prosperity represented in each type of student body.)
5. Subtract the total expense to students from the family-and-student ability to pay to yield the student aid gap which must be filled if the above enrollment assumptions are to be realized. (Moon's seemingly large estimate deals only with the full-time students, however.)

The resultant tables which estimated the 1970 student aid gap are reproduced below.[35]

The resultant total student aid gap for 1970 which emerges at the lower right hand corner of Table II-12, a gap of $3,339,-578,924, is then adjusted downward to $1,903,560,000 on the grounds that this method of projection, if it had been used for the year 1960, would have produced an estimate which was 76 percent higher than the amount of student aid which actually was available in 1960. If the income distribution of students in different kinds of colleges varied this greatly from the model's assumed distribution in 1960, Moon reasoned, the same degree of difference should be also projected for 1970.

Why should a good model framework produce such a large error factor for 1960 (which in turn casts some doubt upon the results for 1970)? As with much projection work, no matter how sophisticated, one may go over the mechanical procedures and assumptions and suggest possible refinements: family incomes (particularly at the higher percentile levels) may be greater than reported in the Census series Moon used, the proportion of full-time students attending college in 1970 may be smaller than Moon's estimates, and so on. Much of this kind of tinkering, however, may arise from an after-the-fact impulse to fudge a reasonable-sounding procedure into yielding reasonable-sounding results. One critically weak assumption in the Moon calculations—critically weak because reliable substitute data was not available to him—is that ". . . by 1970, students in higher education will come from family-income groups in the same proportion as these groups are found in the national population and these students will distribute themselves, again in the same proportion, across the various types of institutions [see Table II-11]." [36]

At first glance, and in the absence of other data, this sounds like a workable statement of a reasonable and democratic goal. However, when tested against the arguments advanced at the beginning of this chapter, and against the calculations in the Tables of Appendix A, the Moon assumption appears unlikely to represent either the events of 1970, or even a moderately realistic goal. Assume, for the moment, that the great majority of the full-time students at Moon's four-year public and four-year private colleges must be able to score 300 or better (roughly the top two-thirds of the nation in measured aptitude) in order to be admitted to these colleges and to survive in the enrollment figures. From the 1969–70 projected table in Appendix A one may estimate the following.

Total number of male and female high school graduates.	2,900,000
Total number able to score 300 or better.	2,012,000
Total number male and female graduates, all score levels, whose family income percentile level is 0–30th percentile.	870,000
Total number, male and female graduates able to score 300 or better *and* whose family income percentile level is 0–30th percentile.	462,000

Moon's model suggests that about 30 percent of the enrollment in each kind of institution might come from the bottom thirty percent of the nation's family income structure. But from the candidate pools derived above from Appendix A, one calculates further that only 23 percent of the high school graduates able to score 300 or better are likely to come from the bottom 30 percent of the family income structure. Because measured student aptitude and family ability to pay do not seem to be totally independent variables, the higher-scoring students tend to cluster at the higher levels of family income. Thus, if one attempts to introduce measured aptitude as an enrollment requirement in Moon's four-year public and private colleges, other assumptions must be added about the behavior of high school

TABLE II-11

Possible distribution of 4,049,734 full-time undergraduate students by family-income level for the year 1970 and their ability to pay for college (Rexford G. Moon model for determining student aid needs for 1970)

Family income [*]	Percentage of family income	Ability to pay	Two-year colleges		Public (four-year)		Private (four-year)	
			Number	Ability to pay	Number	Ability to pay	Number	Ability to pay
$ 2999	8.0	$400	48,597	$ 19,438,800	161,989	$ 64,795,600	113,393	$ 45,357,200
3–3999	4.8	500	29,158	14,579,000	97,194	48,597,000	68,036	34,018,000
4–4999	4.6	870	27,943	13,971,500	93,144	81,035,280	65,201	56,724,870
5–5999	12.4	1150	75,325	37,662,500	251,084	288,746,600	175,759	202,122,850
6–6999	8.2	1430	49,812	24,906,000	166,038	237,434,340	116,227	166,204,610
7–7999	9.9	1565	60,138	30,069,000	200,462	313,723,030	140,323	219,605,495
8–8999	9.9	1745	60,138	30,069,000	200,462	349,806,190	140,323	244,863,635
9–9999	9.9	2215	60,138	30,069,000	200,462	423,375,744	140,323	310,815,445
10–14,999	20.0	2990	121,492	60,746,000	404,973	855,302,976	283,482	847,611,180
15–19,999	9.0	(4440)	54,672	27,336,000	182,238	384,886,656	127,567	448,908,273
20,000–	3.3	(5000)	20,016	10,023,000	66,821	141,125,952	46,774	164,597,706
Total	100.0		607,459	$298,869,800	2,024,867	$3,188,829,368	1,417,408	$2,740,829,264

[*] The income frequencies for the range $7000–9999 and for $10,000 and over were assigned arbitrarily.

TABLE II-12

Total cost of higher education to American families in relation to their total ability to pay for same in the year 1970 (Rexford G. Moon Model for determining student aid needs for 1970)

Type of institution	%	Number of students	Student cost	Total student cost	Ability to pay	Deficit, 1970
Two-year college	15	607,459	$ 500	$ 303,729,500	$ 298,869,800	$ 4,859,700
Public four-year college	50	2,024,867	2112	4,276,519,104	3,188,829,368	1,087,689,736
Private four-year college	35	1,417,408	3519	4,987,858,752	2,740,829,264	2,247,029,488
Total	100	4,049,734		$9,568,107,356	$6,228,528,432	$3,339,578,924

graduates in 1970, if his model still is to stand a chance of proving out satisfactorily. One would have to make one or both of the following possible "corrective" assumptions:

1. That students from low-income families will—at given score levels— enroll in four-year colleges with higher frequency than their higher-income contemporaries.
2. That students from low-income families will drop out of college less frequently than their higher-income contemporaries.

Unfortunately, both of these possible assumptions run directly opposite to recent and to currently foreseeable experience. It seems likely, although the data was never collected to prove or disprove it, that one important reason Moon's model disagreed by a wide margin with actual experience in 1960 was that the socioeconomic mix of students in major groups of American colleges and universities was noticeably unrepresentative of the family income structure in the nation. Notice, in passing, that the direction of apparent error in Moon's assumption here is precisely opposite to the apparent error in market appraisal implied by the 1959 Knox College long-range projections discussed earlier. The initial Knox projections seemed to assume too high a proportion of full-paying (or at least, relatively prosperous) students in the market; Moon assumes too small a proportion. Another element of uncertainty in the Moon projection of aggregate student financial need in 1970 arises because he derives a large adjustment factor for 1970 based on the difference between actual financial aid available to students in 1960 and student financial need projected (by Moon's method) for 1960. While many of the private colleges did award student financial aid in 1960 based on estimates of student financial need (using roughly the same College Scholarship Service estimating procedures which Moon uses for the aggregate projections), it is also true that most of the public colleges did not follow this procedure; these patterns of aid distribution could shift significantly by 1970.

This much time has been devoted to appraising one model of national needs in college student financial aid for a number of reasons. First, it is an early example of many which will probably be put forward as the amount of federal resources devoted to student aid continues to increase; its results seem to suffer not so much from the design of the model's framework as from the scanty data then available to test it and to make it work. Second, the great discrepancy between "calculated" and actual experience in 1960 helps to illustrate here the great degree to which the socioeconomic mix of students in higher education will affect the cost to the nation in maintaining them in college. If all of the difference between Moon's calculated gap in student aid for 1970—$3.3 billion (see Table II-12)—and his adjusted calculation ($1.9 billion) were due to the difference between assumed and actual socioeconomic mix in colleges and universities, then the policy discussion for this factor alone would carry a price tag of 1.4 billion dollars. Although this figure probably represents overstatement of the realistically debatable area, the issue remains important.

In financial terms (leaving aside for the moment the more important considerations of what kind of role our system of higher education is to play in society), this issue has at least two important parts. First, how representative of all kinds of American families do we wish our *whole system* of colleges and universities to be? The answer is affected partly by our wishes as a nation, and partly by the ability, preparation, and desire of students to enter college; as the Moon example illustrates, a nationwide college enrollment that is truly representative of all income levels of families in the United States will be more expensive to maintain than a similar-sized total enrollment in which low-income families are significantly under-represented. Secondly, how representative of all kinds of American families do we wish *individual institutions* to be? If only the rich attend high-cost colleges, and only the poor attend low-cost ones, a given-sized college enrollment, under a need-based system of financial aid to students, can be maintained at the lowest student-aid cost in excess of what parents and students are able to contribute. If this stratified arrangement seems unsatisfactory—which it does—it must be recognized that increasing the degree to which individual colleges enroll students of many backgrounds is also likely to increase the financial cost.

The lack of information which plagued the results of the Moon nationwide model also inhibits accurate illustration of the costs of different degrees of student socioeconomic diversity in individual (or small groups of) institutions. The following approach seems one reasonable way to illustrate this, but all of the figures used in the example are hypothetical, not actual.

Financial aid cost and socioeconomic diversity

Assume, for the moment, a closed system of 10,000 college students, all of whom will attend either an expensive private college, having an enrollment of 5000 and a total cost to a student for a year, including personal expenses of $3500, or a medium-cost residential public college having an enrollment of 5000 and a total cost to a student for a year of $2000. Assume, also, that these 10,000 students come from families whose incomes are today reasonably representative of those now found in colleges of these two kinds. Assume, furthermore, that a three-group family income distribution for these students looks roughly as follows, in Table II-13.

The purpose of setting up this framework is, first, to suggest alternate ways students might be redistributed between these

TABLE II-13

Hypothetical model to illustrate the cost of maintaining different family-income mixtures represented in two colleges (tabulation of initial inputs)

Group	Number of students in each group	Median family income for each group	These students are now distributed in the private and public colleges in this example as follows
I	2000	$17,000	2500 in the private college 500 in the public college
II	5000	8000	2000 in the private college 3000 in the public college
III	2000	4000	500 in the private college 1500 in the public college

two colleges—first, on the assumption that the private college will be forced to economize in its scholarship funds and will therefore compete (successfully) to enroll all of the prosperous students in the model (and also on the assumption that the public college enrollment accommodates the lower-income students displaced from the private college by its economy move); and second, on the opposite assumption that the private college will somehow obtain enough scholarship funds so that it can maintain a more representative student body than before (and that the public college again will adjust accordingly).[37] Then, if either of these shifts in student socioeconomic mix within the system does take place, how much of a cost change would this imply in the costs of direct student financial aid—at each institution and in the system as a whole? Two more columns are added to the model (see Table II-14) to illustrate the two possibilities: Possibility No. 1, towards homogenization of student bodies

TABLE II-14

Hypothetical model: Distribution of students under two different mix assumptions

Group	Number of students in each group	Median family income for each group	Present distribution *	Possibility No. 1, towards homogenization	Possibility No. 2, towards more representative diversity
I	3000	$17,000	Pvt: 2500 Pub: 500	Pvt: 3000 Pub: 0	Pvt: 1500 Pub: 1500
II	5000	8000	Pvt: 2000 Pub: 3000	Pvt: 2000 Pub: 3000	Pvt: 2500 Pub: 2500
III	2000	4000	Pvt: 500 Pub: 1500	Pvt: 0 Pub: 2000	Pvt: 1000 Pub: 1000

* "Pvt." means the number of students in each possible example assumed to be enrolled in the high-cost private college; "Pub." means the number enrolled in the medium-cost public college.

TABLE II-15

Hypothetical model: Cost of distributing students under original and under two different-mix assumptions

Income group (and median income level represented)	Assumed student distribution at present		Possibility No. 1— move towards homogenization of student backgrounds		Possibility No. 2— move towards more representative diversity	
	Number of students	Student aid cost *	Number of students	Student aid cost *	Number of students	Student aid cost *
For the private college:						
I ($17,000)	2500	$ 0,000,000	3000	$ 0,000,000	1500	$ 0,000,000
II ($ 8000)	2000	5,200,000	2000	5,200,000	2500	6,500,000
III ($ 4000)	500	1,650,000	0	0,000,000	1000	3,300,000
Total student aid cost, private college		$ 6,850,000		$ 5,200,000		$ 9,800,000

For the public college:						
I ($17,000)	500	$ 0,000,000	0	$ 0,000,000	1500	$ 0,000,000
II ($ 8000)	3000	3,300,000	3000	3,300,000	2500	2,750,000
III ($ 4000)	1500	2,700,000	2000	3,600,000	1000	1,800,000
Total student aid cost, public college		$ 6,000,000		$ 6,900,000		$ 4,550,000
For the total system:						
Grand total student aid cost (add private and public totals above)		$12,850,000		$12,100,000		$14,350,000

* The cell values for student aid cost were computed as follows. Take, for example, the assumed present student aid cost for maintaining the private-college contingent from income group II (family income median: $8000). Here, one estimates that the total cost to maintain a student in this private college for a year is $3500. There are 2000 students from income group II involved. $3500 × 2000 = $7,000,000, or the total annual cost to these students and their families. From the College Scholarship Service *Financial Aid Manual* one can estimate that an average-sized family with an income of $8000 would be expected to contribute about $900 for the college education of one of the children. Thus, from the total student aid cost of $7,000,000 for this group, one subtracts what the parents might be expected to contribute, or $900 × 2000 = $1,800,000. The remainder, $5,200,000, must be provided in some form of student self-help or outside financial assistance. In other cells, the family contribution from a $17,000 family is about $3500, or close to the private college student expense budget (hence the family is not considered to require financial aid in these calculations); the contribution expected from a family with a $4000 annual income is about $200.

(high-income students increasingly dominate the mix in the high-cost college, while lower-income students predominate in the low-cost college), and Possibility No. 2, towards increasing the representativeness of the student bodies compared with the distribution of income in families through the nation.

Given this kind of information, one may calculate, in much the same way Moon did in his model, the student-aid cost of maintaining these students in college after allowance has been made for what the families may be expected to contribute. Note that this cost calculation says nothing about what the student aid sources will be (institutional, foundation-, industry-, or government-funded) nor what form it will take (scholarship or gift aid, loans, jobs, or contribution from families in excess of expectation); it merely represents a student financial aid cost that must be met somehow, given the starting assumptions.

The cost figures in the cells of Table II-15 represent the student aid cost to someone other than the students' families to maintain the student representatives of each of the three income groups in each of the two colleges, on the basis of calculations for each of the three assumed sets of conditions—initial situation, move towards homogenization, and move towards representativeness in each of the colleges. There are many things wrong with this oversimplified model, of course. Our system of higher education is not "closed" in the sense this model assumed for convenience. If the level of financial aid available generally to students changes, the number of students entering the system probably also changes. Furthermore, the availability of financial aid alone does not determine the flows of students illustrated here; obviously many other elements are important also. All this said, however, the results do suggest that these possible changes in socioeconomic mix would be important both for the financial structure of individual colleges, and for the system as a whole. In the example here, the hypothetical changes suggested for one private college caused the student aid cost, defined in this way, to range from over five to almost ten million dollars. The comparable cost range for the public college was from almost seven million down to four and a half million. Since the shifts were partially offsetting ones, the fluctuation in cost for the whole two-college system was not proportionally as great—but even so the range of cost possibilities for the complete system ranged across an area 18 percent as large as the total cost assumed at the start.[38]

The assumptions used in this model are admittedly arbitrary; however, they seem to be within the range of reason.   They help illustrate the substantial differences in costs associated with different possible student aid policies as they affect diversity or homogeneity of student financial backgrounds within colleges possessing different price structures.   The assumptions in the model would have to contain both gross errors and conveniently offsetting errors before the question of student diversity within different kinds of colleges would cease to be an issue meriting national interest.

Summary

In summary, this chapter has said that colleges need better ways of understanding the consequences—past and future—of their operating decisions in admission policy, in setting the level of expenses their students must meet and in student financial aid policy.   Private colleges, in particular, since they recover a major portion of their operating costs through tuition, need to understand better than they have the market from which they draw this large element of financial support and from which they also draw the students they educate.   The joint distribution of U.S. high school graduates by a nationwide academic measure (verbal score on the Scholastic Aptitude Test) and by a measure of ability to pay (family income) can improve the colleges' understanding in several ways, even though the measuring device is rough and does not take into account many of the other complex elements that also affect a student's choice of college, his survival and accomplishment there, and his performance in later life.

The University of Puget Sound example showed how a college might attempt to use the joint distribution tool to appraise the possible effects on student recruitment of proposed changes in tuition and admission policy.   The Knox College example illustrated how closely an institution's overall planning and its financial health may be linked to the important questions of admission, tuition, and financial aid policy, and how the joint distribution approach may help bring understanding to this group of interrelated elements. The Fisk University example shows how one can use the joint distribution to describe roughly a submarket, the annual population of Negro high school graduates, and how this description can help bring further understanding to the special problems of the predominantly Negro colleges in the United States. The Harvard College example illustrated how the joint distribution can be used to examine different subsegments of an institution's applicant group and enrolled student body: segments defined by different levels of family income and by different levels of measured student aptitude. It illustrated, also, how a college might appraise the potential impact of alternate selection policies upon the national market, as well as appraise its actual impact.

Six groups of colleges were analyzed through the joint distribution approach, for the short period of years when adequate and comparable data was available. This analysis suggests that many of the problems faced by the colleges described in the case-study examples are not atypical, but may have their more or less urgent counterparts throughout American private higher education. Although the necessary supplementary data is not available to analyze thoroughly the impact of these developments upon the public sector, it is clear that it is a substantial one. Two models were presented to comment upon ways of assessing the possible rough magnitude of the problem faced by the federal government if it wishes to provide supplementary, need-based, direct student aid, sufficient to meet whatever definition may be set for universal opportunity for higher education. (The weaknesses in the models served also to illustrate how much more basic data is needed.) Other major forms of government participation, established or potential, in higher education have not been treated in this chapter.

Many simplifications were adopted in setting up and applying the joint distribution tool. These simplifications were necessary in order to make manageable the description of a broad and complex market, and they were also necessary at times because of the limitations of available nationwide data. Undue apology need not be made for this paring-down process, however, since it also brings into focus important relationships which have not appeared as clearly before. The final chapter will set these relationships into a more general perspective.

Notes

[1] Dean W. Seibel, "Prediction of College Attendance," *Vocational Guidance Quarterly*, Summer, 1963, pp. 265–272; *College Board Score Reports* (New York: College Entrance Examination Board, 1963), Table 7, p. 18. William H. Angoff, Executive Associate at Educational Testing Service, has added that other less complete, unpublished information suggests that relationship between test scores and the proportion of the high school population able to achieve various levels of performance on the test has remained relatively stable from about 1950 until the present. Angoff said that both the scoring of the tests, and the questions asked, were sufficiently different before roughly 1950 to render doubtful the validity of the above relationships for analysis of earlier years.

[2] For an excellent critical review of the development of the Scholastic Aptitude Test, see comments contributed by Dean K. Whitla in Oscar K. Buros (ed.), *The Sixth Mental Measurements Yearbook* (Highland Park, N.J.: Gryphon Press, 1965), pp. 974–996.

[3] Selection of only these two variables, while they make the question manageable, ignore other important (but hard to compare on a national basis) kinds of evidence about past or possible future academic performance. Eliminated from the calculated pools are men capable of good academic performance who test badly. Included in the calculated pools are men who do well on tests but who, because of indifference or poor health, perform badly in their work. The two selected variables combined, however, seem to yield a tolerable aggregate measure, even if it would clearly be a wasteful sorting device for operating admission policy. It must also be remembered that by defining the pools as high school graduates, one includes potential college candidates who do not go on to college. This fall-out is relatively small among the very bright and very prosperous but becomes greater than 50 percent at low levels of measured ability and income.

[4] College Scholarship Service, *Financial Aid Manual, 1962–64 Edition, op. cit.*, pp. 43–66. Appendix B illustrates graphically the contribution from family income expected by the College Scholarship Service from families at various income levels and with no unusual drains on their income. (Examples of additional drains for which allowances are made include heavy medical expenses, other children attending private secondary or elementary school, other children attending college, need for additional housekeeping assistance because both parents work, and so on.) The chart is reproduced from the *1964–65 Supplement to the Financial Aid Manual, 1962–64 Edition*, p. 63. It should be noted that this chart has been revised for use in the 1967–68 academic year. The effect of the

revisions is negligible at income levels below roughly $10,000, but is somewhat more lenient towards families in roughly the $13,000-to-$15,000 range. How fully the CSS-member colleges will follow these more generous recommendations remains to be seen.

[5] By interpolation in Appendix A, for the 1961–62 Table, one estimates that a family income of $15,700 represented the 88th percentile level among the nation's family incomes. Thus 12 percent of family incomes could be expected to be at this level or higher.

[6] W. W. Charters, Jr., and N. L. Gage, "Social Class and Intelligence Tests," *Readings in the Social Psychology of Education* (Boston: Allyn and Bacon, 1963), pp. 12–21.

[7] If one uses the 1964 table in Appendix A to check against the empirical National Merit data above, one interpolates in the Appendix A tables (using $r = 0.4$) that for a family income level of $15,000 and a SAT verbal score level of 636, the number of male high school seniors that prosperous *and* that high-testing was roughly 7500—as estimated by the tables. John M. Stalnaker, President of the National Merit Scholarship Corporation, believes that the best guess for that year is closer to 5500 or 6000. It seems as if—at least at this high sector of the joint distribution—the estimates in Appendix A are not only surprisingly close to the empirical information, but for the purposes of this argument anyway, tend to err on the conservative side—if anything overstating the size of candidate pools at each level of joint definition.

[8] Karl Pearson, *Tables for Statisticians and Biometricians, First Edition, Part II* (London: Cambridge University Press, 1931), pp. lii–lxxix, Table VIII (Volumes of Normal Bivariate Surfaces, Positive Correlation) and Table IX (Volumes of Normal Bivariate Surfaces, Negative Correlation). Method of calculation is described in Appendix A.

[9] Similar interpolation in the tables of Appendix A is possible horizontally, to estimate the contraction or expansion of candidate pools for smaller than 50-point increments in SAT scores.

[10] Letter from Richard D. Smith, Vice President, University of Puget Sound, to Humphrey Doermann, January 25, 1966. In this example a family contribution of $1400 was assumed to be necessary for a student to attend the University of Puget Sound in 1965, and $1600 as necessary if the tuition were raised $200.

[11] Dexter M. Keezer (ed.), *Financing Higher Education, 1960–1970* (New York: McGraw-Hill Book Co., 1959), pp. 138–161.

[12] Sidney G. Tickton, "Planning for Institutions of Higher Learning," in Seymour E. Harris (ed.), *Education and Public Policy* (Berkeley, California: McCutchan Publishing Corp., 1965), p. 221.

[13] Information derived from Annual Reports of the Ford Foundation, and quoted in Humphrey Doermann, "Financing Higher Education," *Saturday Review*, November 20, 1965, p. 91; and from conversation with Sidney G. Tickton, October 24, 1963.

[14] Information obtained for worksheets for the "Ashford College Case" and from Walter M. North and Kenneth Brown, *A General Survey of Student*

Assistance at Knox (Office of Student Assistance, Knox College, Galesburg, Illinois, 1964). (Mimeographed.)

[15] Elmer F. Jagow, "Advance Financial Planning for Institutions" in *Student Financial Aid and Institutional Purpose* (New York: College Entrance Examination Board, 1963), p. 82. By 1963–64 the average faculty salary was $9288, slightly above the $9190 which had been projected for that year.

[16] James Cass and Max Birnbaum, *Comparative Guide to American Colleges, 1965 Edition* (New York: Harper and Row, 1965), p. 289.

[17] Dexter M. Keezer (ed.), *Financing Higher Education, 1960–1970, op. cit.,* pp. 138–161; Walter M. North and Kenneth Brown, *A General Survey of Student Assistance at Knox, op. cit.*

[18] Sidney G. Tickton, "Planning for Institutions of Higher Learning," in Seymour E. Harris (ed.), *Education and Public Policy, op. cit.,* p. 232.

[19] Walter M. North and Kenneth Brown, *A General Survey of Student Assistance at Knox, op. cit.,* p. 38.

[20] Assuming a student contributed $335 from his own earnings in 1958–59 and in 1963–64 one can estimate that families might have had to provide $1550 and $2400 to make up the difference without further financial aid from Knox. According to the College Scholarship Service estimating procedures, a normal-budget, three-child family at the 82nd percentile level of U.S. family incomes (families of high school graduates) might have been able to provide $1550 in 1958–59; and a family at the 83rd percentile level in 1963–64 could just have met the $2400 bill.

[21] The doubts one should have are probably greater about the accuracy of this table than about the accuracy of the tables describing all U.S. male high school graduates in Appendix A. There is less supplementary interlocking data available for the Negro population than for the total population with which to test the accuracy of the Negro male high school graduate population estimates which are presented here. These estimates seem to be the most reasonable ones which can be made from the available information, but they need further evaluation and perhaps revision.

[22] Recent studies of the graduation rate for Negro students in Harvard College indicate that it is quite similar to that for the whole student body. A separate study conducted on the performance of Negro students coming from families which received less than $5000 annual income and who enrolled in the classes entering in 1959 through 1961 showed that roughly six out of ten graduated on schedule and roughly seven out of ten graduated within six years of first enrollment; this compares with eight and nine out of ten, respectively for the whole initial enrollment of those classes. The recent experience of classes which are still enrolled in the college suggests that the relative performance of the low-income Negro students is improving, and, if it is surveyed four or six years after initial enrollment, may be closer still to that of the rest of their classmates.

[23] The exclusion of Negro students from the major private colleges in the South is less severe today than when Wright spoke. Wright's main point, however, probably still retains much of its force.

24 In 1962–63 Fisk provided scholarships to 180, or about 18 percent of its students; the average award was about $560. Federal and university loans went to 166 students—roughly a third of them probably also scholarship recipients—averaging about $540 each.

25 Stephen J. Wright, "Financial Aid and the Culturally Deprived," in College Scholarship Service, *Student Financial Aid and Institutional Purpose* (New York: College Entrance Examination Board, 1963), pp. 33–36.

26 James Cass and Max Birnbaum, *Comparative Guide to American Colleges, op. cit.,* pp. 191–192. Tuskegee Institute reported the mean SAT verbal score for its entering class as 302; St. Augustine's College reported a mean score of 301; Morehouse College reported a mean score of 375. Howard University failed to report a mean score, but from rank-in-class information about its students' secondary school records it is possible to estimate reasonably that Howard's mean SAT score could be higher than Fisk's. Howard, however, seems to be the only predominantly Negro college which comes close to Fisk in this respect.

27 See Earl J. McGrath, *The Predominantly Negro Colleges in Transition* (New York: Teachers College Press, Teachers College, Columbia University, 1965), and David Riesman and Christopher Jencks, *The Academic Revolution* (New York: Doubleday and Company, 1968).

28 Compare the trends illustrated in Column 3 versus those in Column 5 in the table; U.S. family incomes (for high school graduates) exceeded Harvard's "no-need" approximate boundary by only $220 in 1955, but exceeded it by $2500 in 1964. The "apparent burden" is the burden apparent under the estimating procedures used prior to 1967–68 by the College Scholarship Service and most of its member colleges; underlying these procedures is the assumption that there is a level of "basic" expense any family faces in bringing up a given number of children, and above that a series of discretionary expenses. It is the discretionary level of expense (or income) which is "taxed" for the family college expense contribution.

29 Often, however, the feedback between predictive measures and selection policy make even this a dubious statement. Imagine a hypothetical university which admitted 600 new students, each with a different SAT score ranging from 200 to 800—the full range of the scale. Even with all the other uncertainties mentioned, a student's SAT scores in the majority of cases would probably predict his relative standing in the university's grading curve tolerably well. There would be exceptions, of course, and some of them quite large. But if the university were to have the chance to select whichever students in the nation it wanted, if its selection committee had learned that in the past the better the applicant's scores the better his college academic performance, and if the selection committee therefore decided to give total weight to measured aptitude in selection—the committee might try to admit only students who had scored 800 on the test.

If the committee succeeded in this ambition, and if meanwhile the university maintained some differentiation in the academic grades it assigned student work, the committee by its success would also have destroyed completely the apparent predictive ability of the selection variable it was relying on: if all entering students had the same score, but then earned different grades in college, the predictive power of an 800 score would be gone. The beginning and ending point of this hypothetical sequence of selection policies are both unrealistically extreme, but the reduced predictive power of this kind of variable after selection policy has consciously truncated it—without comparable adjustment in the later performance-measurement scale—is real indeed at many colleges across the country.

[30] The percentage of Harvard freshmen with honor averages (Dean's List) at the end of freshman year was: for the Class of 1968, 51.5 percent; for the Class of 1967, 47.4 percent, and for the Class of 1966, 47.3 percent. The ten-year average for the Classes of 1959 through 1968 was 44.2 percent.

[31] Quoted from the award description of the David McCord Prize.

[32] One could argue that the score distribution in these colleges was already remarkably high at the beginning period of the comparison. Student expense budgets were obtained from the *College Handbook 1961–63* and *College Handbook 1963–65* published by the College Entrance Examination Board and adjusted, where necessary, to be roughly comparable as to expense items included.

[33] U.S. Office of Education, *Digest of Educational Statistics, 1963* (Washington: U.S. Government Printing Office, 1963), Table 30, p. 41. While it does not affect the size of the pools as defined here, it is also true that in this period the percentage of high school graduates going on to higher education also increased.

[34] Rexford G. Moon, Jr., "Determining Aid Needs for 1970: A Model," *College Board Review*, Vol. 54 (Fall 1964). (New York: College Entrance Examination Board, 1964), pp. 11–15.

[35] *Ibid.*, p. 13.

[36] *Ibid.*, p. 12.

[37] Note also that the public college in this example is assumed to be awarding financial aid on the basis of student financial need, which is not the common practice for most public colleges today. However, the large new federal scholarship program does operate on a need basis, which in turn, is moving every U.S. college which participates in the federal programs at least one step towards this method of operation.

[38] $\dfrac{\$14,350,000 - \$12,100,000}{\$12,850,000} = 18$ percent.

III

The Market Perspective

As late as in the year 1964, the best available projection of total enrollment in U.S. colleges and universities for the fall of 1965 was an estimate of 5,220,000 students. In December 1965 the U.S. Office of Education reported that the actual total enrollment was 5,570,000—some 6.7 percent larger than the earlier estimates.[1]

In May, 1963, John F. Morse, Executive Associate of the American Council on Education, reminded his audience at the College Scholarship Service Colloquium in Excelsior Springs, Missouri:

> You must remember that although seven years is not a long time, the character of student financial aid has changed radically since those days. It was known then, for example, that students would not borrow for an education. It was known that the public would not put up with basing the size of scholarship stipends on a means test if those stipends came from tax funds. Although the College Scholarship Service had come into existence, it was known that there was no way of measuring with any degree of accuracy an applicant's financial need. All kinds of things were known which have since proved untrue.[2]

Any attempt to forecast the future size and form of an enterprise as diverse as higher education in the United States is almost certainly destined to be incorrect. Forecasts do have some usefulness, however. One kind of use was illustrated for an individual college in the Knox College example of Chapter II, as a rough benchmark by which to appraise later changes. In this chapter, the forecasts of enrollment illustrate a reasonable range of guesses about important parts of the market for higher education in the next decade. This seems necessary to make clearer the assumptions and judgments underlying much of the work presented in the first two chapters.

EXPANSION OF DEMAND FOR POST-SECONDARY EDUCATION

Probably the most important and, apparently, the most predictable element of change foreseeable in the market for higher education in the United States is the expansion of total demand. The most frequently used projections of total degree-credit enrollment in American colleges and universities suggest that possibly by 1980, and certainly by 1985, the nation will fill as many new places in American higher education as were created during our whole previous history. If a general war comes upon us, or if the trends in the rising generation reverse themselves—so that a higher proportion drops out of elementary and secondary schooling or desires *not* to attend college after high school—or if those allocating resources in higher education take a new and much more restrictive view about investment in new capacity for the system, then the higher education enrollment projections now in fashion could fail to be realized, by wide margins. All of these "ifs," however, run contrary to the experience of the past twenty years; while any one, or any combination, is possible, none seem to represent what one would predict today, if limited to a single best guess.

However, it seems unlikely that this doubling of enrollment, if it occurs, will serve merely to double the elements present in our college and university system today. While some of the enrollment increase will be due to population increase and hence might be expected to include a similar distribution of talent, ambition, and financial resources as immediately preceding classes, a considerable portion of the new increment will probably be a result of reduced dropping out at earlier levels of schooling. The new potential college enrollees from this source are likely to be predominantly students in the middle ranges of measured aptitude, and, compared with today's college students, they will be both less anxious and less able to pay for completing four years of college, let alone postgraduate education. Meanwhile, the demand in the labor force for larger numbers of professional and highly skilled workers seems likely to continue to expand general student demand for four years of undergraduate college and also for postgraduate training. If the trends of the last ten years continue for the next ten, one may expect growth in all of the major classifications of higher education, with the most rapid enrollment expansion occurring in the two-year colleges and the graduate schools, and significant, but less rapid expansion taking place in the four-year colleges. All this, in turn, makes no mention of wholly new patterns of higher education or new kinds of institutions, which may arise, but for which there is now no precedent.

Table III-1 below summarizes the total degree-credit enrollment growth anticipated by the U.S. Office of Education in the major components of American higher education between 1965 and 1975. During this period, total estimated enrollment, based on the trend in enrollment patterns set up between 1954 and 1964 and applied to the population now passing through elementary and secondary school, is expected to increase 64 percent, while enrollment in four-year undergraduate colleges, two-year colleges, and graduate schools are expected to increase 58 percent, 75 percent, and 89 percent respectively.

In March, 1963, Professor Harold Wolozin of American University prepared a set of projections for the Fund for the Advancement of Education which estimated, among other elements, the distribution of college and university students among public and private institutions from 1965 to 1985. These projections are compared in Table III-2 with those prepared by the U.S. Office of Education. The enrollment totals for the whole system of U.S. higher education generated in each set of estimates are quite similar; while neither set fully anticipated the size of

TABLE III-1

Projected total fall degree-credit enrollment in U.S. higher education by type and level of institution, 1965 and 1975 (U.S. Office of Education estimates) *

Year	Total degree-credit fall enroll-ment	Four-year under-graduate college enrollment	Two-year college enrollment	Graduate school enroll-ment
1965	5,435,000	4,067,000	791,000	577,000
1975	8,918,000	6,440,000	1,386,000	1,092,000
Percent change 1965–75	+64	+58	+75	+89

* U.S. Office of Education, *Projections of Educational Statistics to 1974–75*, *op. cit.*, Tables 5, 8, and 10. The projections in these tables extend only to 1974; in order to generate figures comparable to the Wolozin projections for the Fund for the Advancement of Education, the U.S. Office of Education estimates were projected forward an additional year.

the enrollment jump which took place between 1964 and 1965, or another one which occurred in 1966, the U.S. Office of Education figures start higher (closer to the 5.57 million actual enrollment in 1965) and remain larger by the same amount through the ten years in which they can be compared. However, Professor Wolozin made larger allowance than did the U.S. Office of Education for the effect that the increasing public-private tuition differentials might have in shifting the balance of enrollment towards the public sector. The U.S. Office of Education projected the public-private enrollment distribution based on the trend of attendance rates established between 1954 and 1964 and applied these to an anticipated population aged 18 through 21.

It is possible to make at least a reasonable guess that the U.S. Office of Education projections represent a minimum rate of change likely in the distribution of students between public

TABLE III-2

Projected total fall degree-credit enrollment in U.S. higher education by type of control: U.S. Office of Education estimates 1965–75 and Fund for the Advancement of Education estimates 1965–85 *

Year	U.S. Office of Education					Fund for the Advancement of Education				
	Total enrollment	Public	Public percentage of total	Private	Private percentage of total	Total enrollment	Public	Public percentage of total	Private	Private percentage of total
1965	5435	3519	64.7	1916	35.3	5220	3341	64.0	1879	36.0
1970	7225	4815	66.6	2410	33.4	7003	4693	67.0	2310	33.0
1975	8918	6109	68.5	2809	31.5	8667	6241	72.0	2426	28.0
1980						10,006	7505	75.0	2501	25.0
1985						12,840	10,272	80.0	2568	20.0
Percentage change 1965–75:	+64	+74		+47		+66	+87		+29	
Percentage change 1965–85:						+146	+207		+37	

*U.S. Office of Education, *Projections of Educational Statistics to 1974–75*, op. cit., Tables 5 and 14; Harold Wolozin, *The Outlook for Higher Education*, op. cit., pp. 20, 21.

and private colleges, that the Wolozin figures represent a best-guess projection, and that unless the trends in tuition-and-fee increases cease diverging between public and private colleges, the shift towards the public sector could be even more rapid. This acceleration, in turn, could be partially or fully offset by substantial increases in the private sector of direct financial aid (or some other effective subsidy) for students who cannot pay the full cost of attending.

Both the U.S. Office of Education estimates and those of Wolozin assume that the total number of students going on to college will increase as a combined result of two trends: substantially rising numbers of high school graduates, and a slowly increasing college entrance rate among high school graduates—both trends determined by the experience of recent prior years. Daniel Patrick Moynihan points out that if a massive federal effort were to provide both financial assistance to students from low and middle-income families and greatly expanded community college facilities—particularly in relatively low-income regions—the proportion of high school graduates going on to further education could by 1970 conceivably be as high as 66.7 percent (compared with the 55.4 percent projected for that year by the U.S. Office of Education). Moynihan believes that by 1970 this would represent as great a step as feasible towards universal opportunity for higher education. (The other third of the nation's high school graduates, he estimates, probably do not have the wish or the ability to continue formal education productively past high school.)

Moynihan's "universal opportunity" projection for the national freshman class in 1970 is compared below, in Table III-3, with the comparable estimate made by the U.S. Office of Education.

Other projection studies have attempted to appraise whether faculty of sufficient quality and quantity can be found to teach as many new students as the commonly-used enrollment projects anticipate. Some studies, like Moynihan's, inquire as to the possible effects on the national economy if so many young men and women are drawn off so quickly from the labor force. Still

TABLE III-3

U.S. Office of Education projection of first-time opening fall degree-credit enrollment in all institutions of U.S. higher education, 1965 and 1970, compared with D. P. Moynihan "universal opportunity" first-time enrollment estimate for 1970 *

Year	U.S.O.E. projected first-time enrollment	Percentage of U.S. high school graduates same year	D. P. Moynihan projected first-time enrollment	Percentage of U.S. high school graduates same year
1965	1,445,000	53.2	1,445,000 (U.S.O.E.)	53.2 (U.S.O.E.)
1970	1,614,000	55.4	1,947,000	66.7
Percentage of change 1965 to 1970	+12		+35	

* U.S. Office of Education, *Projections of Educational Statistics to 1974–75*, Tables 5, 8. First-time students are beginning freshmen, part-time or full-time, with no prior credits applicable towards a bachelor's degree. Also Daniel Patrick Moynihan, "The Impact on Manpower Development and Employment of Youth" in Earl J. McGrath (ed.), *Universal Higher Education, op. cit.*, 1966, pp. 78, 85.

others, referred to briefly earlier, have attempted to cost out the whole enterprise to see whether the nation can possibly afford it.[3] Expansion of this magnitude will certainly be difficult; but with tolerable revisions to our national spending priorities (except possibly in the event of global war when the supply of students might also be cut off) and perhaps with tolerable compromises in teacher qualifications in parts of the system, these projection studies do not raise serious questions about the nation's capacity to meet any of the levels of student demand suggested above.

The first and central assumption made about the next ten years in American higher education, then, is that they will call for tremendous expansion of student capacity under most foreseeable combinations of circumstances. Much of this demand will appear in public institutions, occasioned by students of middling academic aptitude, prior academic performance, and ability to pay. Some of the new demand will be merely an extension of present demand, expanded as the college-age population grows, and some may arise from the new demands of adults several years out of high school. With such a revolution in demand taking place—which will occur, probably, at the same time that the pace of technological change is accelerating—one could suggest that revolution has become a habit and that within the next ten years the structure of American higher education will be so altered as to make the concerns of the first three chapters virtually obsolete. If, for example, admission, tuition, and student financial aid policy ceases to be controlled primarily at the institutional (college) level (as opposed, say, to the federal level), or if our pattern of control for colleges and universities ceased to be a mixed, public *and* private one with separate patterns of pricing and admission criteria, or if tuition charges to students ceased to be relatively important to the financing of American colleges (particularly the private ones), then much of the previous chapters, while still helpful in understanding the early postwar history of American higher education, would be irrelevant for helping to plan its future. But these three elements—institutional-level policy control, a mixed system of public and private control, and a student fee structure which makes relatively high financial demands (compared with other countries and with other levels in American education) on families which can afford to pay for college—have served us well, though obviously without perfection. All of these elements are undergoing change. It is possible that the next ten years will see one, or all disappear, but this study and the projections in this chapter proceed on more conservative assumptions. These assumptions are that these elements will not, and probably should not change so rapidly as to be unrecognizable by 1975. By then, one may hope, we will have experimented successfully with, and begun to fund adequately, new kinds of institutions dealing with vocational education, adult education, as well as perhaps the traditional questions of liberal arts and preprofessional education in new ways. This study has been primarily concerned, then, not with what may become the leading edge of new developments in American higher education, but with the problem of enabling important parts of the present system to remain as flexible as possible and more intelligently responsive to environmental change. The design of the leading edge is critically important, but it is a problem different enough in nature to have remained intentionally outside the scope of this study, given the assumptions above.

INSTITUTIONAL CONTROL OF OPERATING POLICY IN HIGHER EDUCATION

Frank H. Bowles, former president of the College Entrance Examination Board and currently Advisor on International Education to the Ford Foundation, points out that roughly three-fourths of the world's educational systems (enrolling roughly half the world's college and university students) select students for higher education at the secondary school level rather than at the point of admission to college, or later, as happens in the United States. Only about a quarter of the countries of the world (the United States and the Soviet Union are among them) place the selection responsibility upon the individual institutions of higher education.[4]

In selecting students for higher education (leaving aside, for the present, motivation, ability to pay, and other elements of self-selection by potential candidates), most nations use the results of subject matter examinations as the sole or dominant criterion. The United States is virtually alone in making important use of academic aptitude tests, secondary school grades, interview information, and other kinds of evidence about its candidates for college.[5] Within the United States, of course, the elements considered for admission to particular kinds of colleges vary enormously. But United States college administrators and faculty committees do have in combination a greater responsibility for selecting who is admitted, and they have available more different kinds of student information that may be considered relevant selection evidence than is generally true elsewhere in the world. The recent increase in federal and state legislation, to give financial aid to particular kinds of students and offer to finance particular kinds of training programs adds qualifications to this generalization, but does not alter the main point.

Furthermore, the United States provides higher education for an unusually large proportion of its population and accommodates in its college and university admissions process, taken as a whole, an unusually wide range of preparation and academic ability. More than in many countries, American elementary schools, secondary schools, and many colleges have provided a "second chance" kind of flexibility which permits students to move relatively quickly into programs which are most appropriate for them.[6] This does not overlook the distressingly frequent examples one finds of rigid schools, inappropriate placement, and smothered opportunity, but this does suggest that the variety of candidates planning on higher education and the variety of routes by which they approach college and, later, college graduation in America, has been unusually great compared with most of the rest of the world.

The extent to which the United States educational system fails to provide sufficient opportunity represents a tangled cluster of questions and definitions which seems to defy general agreement. Dael Wolfle has estimated that in 1953, of all U.S. high school graduates with aptitude scores equal to those of the average entering college freshmen (scores which also placed them in about the top 40 percent of the high-school-graduate score distribution), only 40 percent were actually going on to college. Daniel Patrick Moynihan, using Project TALENT data, estimated that by 1961 roughly 70 percent of the comparable group was entering college within a year of graduation from high school.[7] To the extent that these studies are comparable (the Wolfle study design was not readily available to test comparability), they represent strong testimony of the degree to which American higher education broadened and extended its reach in the 1950's.

Bowles contrasts the provisions made for identifying and training students of superior ability in the United States with the kinds of provisions made in other major educational systems.

Three approaches to provision for students of superior ability may be identified.

1. In some systems, specific efforts are made to identify such pupils early in their education, to give them special attention and to provide extra opportunities for them, sometimes including financial aid. Various forms of this approach may be observed in the Soviet Union, the United Kingdom, and the United States, where primary and secondary schools are expected to identify students of unusual ability. Programmes of advanced studies are available for such students in many, though not all, schools in these systems.   As these students progress through secondary school, arrangements may be made for them to move directly into certain advanced studies while still in secondary school, as in the United States; or to enter higher education without being required to fulfill the two-year work requirements, as in the Soviet Union; or to compete for especially choice scholarships, as in the United Kingdom.

2. In other systems, there is interest in the identification of such students and encouragement for them to proceed at their own pace. They are also allowed to advance into higher education one or two years ahead of the normal entering age, but no special programmes of study are provided for them.   This approach may be observed in some European countries, particularly France.

3. In the majority of systems, however, no special effort is made to identify students of unusual ability.   No special programmes or privileges are provided for them, nor are they given any opportunity to advance more rapidly or further in their studies than their fellows. This complete lack of special provision for gifted students is characteristic of systems which operate entirely in terms of examination requirements throughout the admissions process.[8]

If one accepts this testimony as reliable, American higher education has not a bad record of performance in the flexible placement of a relatively large proportion of our college-age population in appropriate institutes, colleges, and universities. One may argue that a much more centralized system ought to be able to do the job better, but there do not seem to be major examples elsewhere in the world that provide transferable and convincing evidence.   This of course does not end the debate, but it does seem to shift the burden of proof.

MIXED PUBLIC AND PRIVATE CONTROL IN U.S. HIGHER EDUCATION

College education in the United States, also, is personally financed far more by students and their families than either primary and secondary education, or than higher education in most other countries; and the control of colleges and universities in the United States is far closer to the individual institutions than it tends to be in Europe and in most parts of the world.[9] In this combination of circumstances, decisions of American college administrators and faculties about tuition and financial aid policy have far greater effect on the structure of American higher education (and how students with varying financial resources distribute themselves throughout the system) then can be true at other levels of education in the United States, or in higher education elsewhere. Whether this combination of circumstances is or is not the best possible combination has been debated frequently, and no doubt will continue to be. The ideal may be debatable; the present fact is not.

The following Tables III-4 and III-5 illustrate the extent to which enrollment in the United States shifts between the secondary and higher-education levels from being predominantly within public control to being within a mixture of public and private control. Although student enrollment in public colleges and universities is larger than in private ones, and is also growing faster, there are still more private institutions than public.

The dominant financing pattern in United States elementary and secondary education is the pattern of the neighborhood public school: tuition-free, supported mainly by local property tax revenues, supplemented by state and federal funds. Tuition fees are charged in most public colleges and universities, however, but compared with those in private colleges, they are low, particularly for in-state residents. Other than the subsidy implied by low tuition, however, undergraduate student gift aid from public funds has, until recently, been negligible and is still small. The most notable exception to this came during the period after

TABLE III-4

Number of public and nonpublic high school graduates (1963–64)
and number of first-time enrollments in U.S. higher education (1965),
public and nonpublic *

	Number of high school graduates (1963–64)	Number of first-time enrollments in higher education (1964)
Public institutions	2,020,680	819,622
Nonpublic institutions	274,948	415,184

* U.S. Office of Education, *Digest of Educational Statistics, 1965 Edition* (Washington: U.S. Government Printing Office, 1965), Tables 36, 52. First-time students are beginning freshmen, full-time or part-time, with no prior credits applicable towards a bachelor's degree.

World War II when veterans received education grants through the G.I. Bill.

Private colleges usually charge more (although rarely the full cost of instruction), and then remit some of the tuition income in scholarship awards to students who cannot afford the full charges. Private college tuition and total charges to students are both rising faster than the corresponding public college fees.[10]

John F. Morse, Director of the Commission on Federal Relations of the American Council on Education, in 1964, while advocating stronger federal support of college student financial aid programs, made the following comment.

During the course of my study last year for Representative Edith Green's subcommittee on education, a number of things struck me with particular force. One was the largely unplanned anomaly in which we as a nation provide free education for all through grade 12 and for most who are capable of it after grade 16, while at the same time we mark off four years as a sink-or-swim period and let those who are strong enough to do it on their own resources attempt the passage. . . .[11]

TABLE III-5

United States institutions of higher education by institutional control and highest level of offering, 1960–61 *

Type of control	Highest level of offering					
	2 to 4 years beyond 12th grade	Bachelors' &/or first profes- sional degrees	Masters' &/or second prof.	Ph.D. or equiv- alent	Other degrees	Total
Public:						
State	38	94	162	93	6	393
District or city	308	4	9	6	1	328
Private:						
Independent of church	115	183	124	71	19	512
Protestant	84	271	92	23	5	475
Roman Catholic	45	181	65	16	1	308
Other	3	8	3	10	–	24
Total	593	741	455	219	32	2040

* Dr. A. H. Halsey, Sir John Cockcroft, Professor Ingvar Svennilson, *Higher Education and the Demand for Scientific Manpower in the United States* (Paris: O.E.C.D., 1963), p. 23.

The extent to which colleges in the United States rely on student income is illustrated in Table III-6, which provides British figures for comparison. Great Britain's institutions of higher education, in turn, seem to derive a relatively large share of their income from student fees, when compared with the other major European systems.[12]

The 1957 and 1958 current income figures for colleges and universities in the United States and Great Britain are the most recent ones which are both comparable and readily available. In passing, one may note that the more recent United States statistics from the U.S. Office of Education show that by 1963–64, student fees had become a slightly smaller proportion of educa-

TABLE III-6

Percentage distribution of current income of institutions of higher learning in United States (1957–58) and Great Britain (1958–59) by source of income *

Source of Income	United States	Great Britain
Student fees	25.0	12.3
Government		
National	18.9⎱	
State	30.7⎰	67.1
Local	3.4	2.6
Endowments, etc.	13.5	8.0
Other	8.5	10.0
Total	100.0	100.0

* Dennis S. Lees, "Financing Higher Education in the United States and Britain," in Selma J. Mushkin (ed.), *Economics of Higher Education* (Washington: U.S. Government Printing Office, 1962), Table 1, p. 330.

tional and general income than in 1957–58: 24.2 percent (in 1963–64) compared with 25.0 percent in 1957–58. In American private colleges, tuition and fees represented (in 1963–64) 37.7 percent of educational and general income, and in the public colleges, 13.7 percent.

The figures for the United States and for Great Britain only summarize payments to institutions, however. Neither set of figures shows government payments to students toward their maintenance in universities. Roughly three-quarters of the British university students received public grants which paid at least their full student fees. United States students received some veterans' benefits, some special purpose federal grants, and some state scholarships, but not on any scale currently approaching the British experience.[18]

So far this particular section has described briefly how U.S. higher education differs both from other levels of education in the United States and from other major systems of higher education in the world first, in that the sector of private control is proportionately much larger, and second, in that United States students and their families pay a relatively large share both of the total price of higher education (defined as an all-expense cost to students of attending college for a year) and of the total costs (as colleges and universities finance them) of that education. What follows is an analysis of why these characteristics of American higher education—which to many seem both untidy and wasteful—may be worth trying to preserve for reasons other than mere expediency.

William G. Bowen, Professor of Economics at Princeton University, provides a provocative summary of the effect which heavy reliance on student fees has had on the structure of American higher education, and of why, perhaps, the British experience has been different.

While all of the figures needed to permit an accurate comparison of the shares of the gross national products devoted to higher education in the two countries are not readily available, the qualitative conclusion that the U.S. spends significantly more than Britain is generally accepted. The question for discussion here is not in which country (if either) the "right" share is being spent, but rather what roles have been played by the alternative methods of finance in determining the existing inter-country differences.

In trying to answer this question quantitatively, one would, of course, have to allow for inter-country differences in the level of real income per capita, in income distribution, in the marginal productivity of educational expenditures, and in "tastes" for education. Even at the purely conceptual level (where one can allow himself the luxury of abstracting from these "other" determinants), the question of the relation between methods of finance and total expenditures is too involved to be gone into in detail here. All I can do is offer a few general observations and then try to relate these observations to the actual situation in Britain and the United States.

The first general point is that university education generates what the economist calls "external economies" or "social benefits." That is, the activities of a university confer indirect benefits on the populace as a whole as well as direct benefits on individual students. University education presumably facilitates the processes of democratic government and increases the stock of scientific knowledge (which in turn permits technological progress)—to cite only two out of a very diverse group of community benefits.[14]

One aspect of the relation between social benefits, methods of finance, and total educational spending can be stated as follows: If a country finances its university system solely by means of student charges, with each student paying the full costs of his education, then the total amount of university education demanded will fall short of the optimal level because not all students will include the community benefits of education in their own benefit/cost calculations. A financing system which includes a provision for some type of government grant will, on this count alone, tend to lead to larger expenditures for education because the existence of community benefits will enter into decisions as to the amounts of public grants.[15]

However, while social benefit considerations suggest that more educational expenditures will result from a pure grant system (with no fees charged to students at all) than from a pure fee system, other considerations suggest the opposite conclusion. Education, of course, confers significant direct benefits on the students themselves (ranging from potentially higher lifetime earnings and more attractive jobs to the immediate pleasures of "college days" and increased long-term ability to enjoy leisure time), and taxpayers as a group may well object to paying the full cost of something which benefits particular individuals so directly. To put the point in a provocative form, why should the public at large pay the full costs of educating a girl of only ordinary ability whose primary reason for going to college is to enjoy herself?

Whatever our personal answer to this question, it is certainly clear that a majority of taxpayers might vote against such an expenditure. But, if we were operating under a fee system, and if the girl were willing to pay for her college education just as she might spend money for other goods and services such as cars and vacations, she would presumably have this option. The point is, given sufficient direct personal benefits, the sum total of private demands for higher education may exceed the amount of education that society will pay for out of general tax revenues.

A "mixed" system consisting of a combination of government grants and private fees seems likely, in most circumstances, to result in larger educational expenditures than either of the "pure" systems. The government grants can be used to make sure that expenditures are pushed far enough to take advantage of the social benefits. At the same time, students who are willing and able to pay a share of the costs of their education can be expected to do so, thus reducing taxpayer opposition to the idea of public handouts to students.

Applying these observations to Britain and the U.S., it is apparent, first of all, that the U.S. financing system is considerably more "mixed" than the British. When we recall that in the British case not only are fees low, but the government pays the bulk of fees anyway (and the bulk of maintenance costs as well), it is apparent that British students and their families pay an exceedingly small share of the total costs of university education. My own suspicion is that the limited access of British universities to private funds helps explain the somewhat smaller share of the national product spent on higher education in Britain and that without some increase in private charges it is going to be difficult to raise this share appreciably. . . .

A system in which fees constitute a significant fraction (say 50%) of the educational and general costs of education (excluding large-scale organized research expenditures) has at least two important advantages. First, the universities are provided with a source of unrestricted funds, which they can spend as they like, and which depend only on their ability to persuade prospective students that they are offering good educational value. Second, people in general are given a more realistic idea of the true costs of higher education; and therefore decisions to expand, to subsidize the education of some students, and so on, can be made on the basis of more direct knowledge of what is required in the way of resources.

Generous scholarship programs and other forms of student aid (covering living expenses as well as fees) are essential if we are to make sure that our most promising students, regardless of their ability to pay, are given the opportunity of receiving the best available education. In my judgment the U.S. has not gone far enough in this direction. . . . Britain, on the other hand, seems to me to have gone too far along the scholarship-plus-maintenance-grant-for-everyone route. . . .

The reader may object that in the case of both Britain and the U.S. I am arguing for many-faced financing systems which include general-purpose government grants, sponsored research funds, scholarship money, and direct student payments, and that in this way I am refusing to make choices. I accept the "many-faced" characterization, but I reject the inference that multiple sources imply unprincipled compromise. Economists are always talking about combinations of inputs and diminishing returns, and I believe that this is a clear case in which it is quite possible to rely too heavily on any one source of finance. Mixed solutions may at first blush seem to some to be intellectually messy; but they often make practical sense, and at a deeper level they can be intellectually satisfying as well.[16]

Bowen, for the most part, is contrasting the apparent differences resulting from different financing patterns in British and United States higher education. Except in the last two paragraphs, he does not enter the debate as to what financing patterns would be most likely to produce optimum results for either system. There is a growing body of economic research and prescription, however, which does attempt to bring the tools of welfare economics and pricing theory to bear on this question. Starting with different assumptions and different assumed goals for higher education, the prescriptions which economists have put forward in recent years inevitably differ greatly. Milton Friedman, Professor of Economics at the University of Chicago, has proposed that student fees should cover much more of the costs of higher education in the United States than they do at present.[17] John Vaizey, of Oxford University, has sharply disagreed; in Vaizey's view a student fee system is at best a temporary expedient, and the existence of a substantial, privately-controlled sector in higher education has, in the long view, very little reason for existence.[18] Standing between these extreme views are major contributions by Gary S. Becker, Theodore W. Schultz, Edward F. Denison, and Seymour E. Harris, to name only a few. While their work differs in many other respects, most of these men (Friedman perhaps excepted) would probably agree that further expansion of the United States system of higher education is important both to the economy and to the structure of American society, that more resources (a larger proportion of a rising Gross National Product) should somehow be committed to this expansion, and that in the foreseeable future, a peacetime or limited-war United States economy should, by a relatively mild reordering of its spending priorities, be able to afford the new levels of expense involved.

COMMENTS ON PERSPECTIVE AND METHOD

The foregoing sections of this chapter presented the main elements of perspective that played an important part in the design of this study. The salient elements were: first, estimates of future enrollment in American colleges and universities, which imply unprecedented growth over a relatively short period, and second, characteristics of institutional control and funding which will almost surely encounter great pressures during this expansion, which may undergo change, but which nonetheless seem relatively durable even though new patterns may also appear alongside the old and may eventually have great effect upon them.

If the control of operating policies of colleges in admissions, tuition, and student financial aid are likely, at least in important part, to remain decentralized, at or near the institutional level, then it seems important to design methods of analysis which may be helpful in assessing policy at the institutional level, as well as at a broader level. The joint distribution of measured aptitude and family income is designed to help meet this need. If students (and their families) in important segments of higher education are to be asked to pay a relatively large share of the costs of that education, then it is important to take account both of their ability to pay, and also of their probable ability to do the work required. If one of the critical needs of colleges generally in the next decade is to be able to respond intelligently to the sharply changing numbers of students seeking admission, then it is important to try to devise methods which help individual colleges to make rough appraisals, ahead of time, of their proposed policies in admissions, tuition, and financial aid—and so help take at least some of the burden from the present means of decision-making, which tends to rely on intuition, inspection of what the immediate competition is doing, and then trial and error. Too much should not be claimed for the power of the joint distribution tool, however. Many more elements are important to policy formation in admissions, tuition, and financial aid than one rough measure of academic aptitude and one measure of ability to pay; these elements are in turn intimately related to many other policy areas, of which curriculum design, overall financial planning, and the relationship of colleges to the distribution of talent in society only begin the list.

The findings of this study and the issues that they raise are also related (sometimes in unexpected ways) to the overall perspective outlined earlier in this chapter and in Chapter I. While we have come to think of rising enrollment demands becoming a fixture of the environment for American colleges in the next decade, the study makes clear that some of the most selective and academically rigorous of these colleges, through their admission policies, are actually narrowing sharply the effective pools of candidates from which they draw each year, often to a far greater extent than many of them realize. The competition for the ablest of these students (and particularly in turn for the most prosperous of these) is more intense than is generally realized. Even allowing for considerable error in these estimates, they appear to place greater limitation upon the freedom of most private colleges both to raise minimum aptitude score qualifications (and/or rank-in-class qualifications) for admission and also to increase student expense budgets faster than family incomes rise.

To the extent that colleges and universities enjoying a strong market position compete more aggressively for the bright and the prosperous students, and to the extent at the same time the cost gap between private colleges and nearby public colleges grows, the pressure seems likely to be great indeed both on the financial structure of many private colleges and consequently on the long-run quality of instruction they are able to offer.

Perhaps most of these institutions will be able to marshal sufficient resources from their traditional sources of income. From all that has been said here, this does not seem likely without requiring unwanted compromises in the academic ability and socioeconomic diversity of the students enrolled, or in the quality of programs offered, or in both.[19]

If all of this correctly outlines one of the major problems developing in American higher education, it seems clear not only that these colleges face increased pressure to reach optimum decisions about admission, tuition, and financial aid policy, but that federal and state legislatures, to the extent they are called on for supplementary resources, will need more and better information about what is happening to their present contributions, how much more is needed for what purposes, and how these needs may be met with minimum damage to institutional autonomy (or to the advantages of decentralized control of educational and institutional policy throughout the system as a whole). Worthwhile beginnings have been made, but much more needs to be done.

The issues raised in this study for the most part have been brought up and treated as they appear at the various points of decision in colleges and in government bodies. They overflow untidily across the rough boundaries of several of the academic disciplines in the social sciences. To what extent is student ability to score well on aptitude tests related to family income? Is this a question for educational psychologists, for sociologists, for economists, or for all of them? How do the growth trends in variously defined candidate pools affect the ability of individual colleges and groups of colleges to fulfill their overall educational purposes and to see that their programs are adequately funded? Is this a question for educators, for economists, for students of political science, or some combination of the three? How can state and federal governments, if they are interested in designing efficient programs of supplementary direct student financial aid, devise measurements which will help them determine how great is the gap between the accomplishments of present student aid programs of all kinds, and the accomplishments which one might define as desirable goals for state or national policy? Is this, again, an educator's question, an economist's, or a political scientist's? How strong is the justification for using primarily "objective" academic criteria for selecting students for higher education? Is this primarily an issue of educational psychology, or sociology, of politics (broadly defined)—or what? How concerned should we be, as a matter of national policy, that our college enrollment pattern by 1985 seems likely to shift so predominantly into the public sector? The issues raised (and the list above is only a partial one) are broad, important, and deserve more inquiry and attention than the time and resources available here have been able to bring to bear. One hopes that this further inquiry will be improved by informed attention from the many general and specialized viewpoints concerned, and not merely from one or two.

FLEXIBILITY IN AMERICAN HIGHER EDUCATION

How can the United States manage to maintain flexible diversity in the paths by which students eventually place themselves in society? This insistent question helped to give rise to this study, and, still largely unanswered, ends it. André L. Danière notes, in *Higher Education in the American Economy*, a similar view to that of Frank Bowles earlier in this chapter.

If there is anything unique about American higher education it is the flexibility of the system, its willingness and ability to absorb men and women who did not necessarily take the right degrees, in the right order, and at the right age.[20]

Fred L. Glimp, former Dean of Admissions and Financial Aids in Harvard College, notes, however, that as the pressures of expanding enrollment impinge on public and private colleges the signs of rigidity, not increased flexibility, begin to appear.

In the public state and city universities, it has always been an article of faith that higher education should be available to all students who can qualify. The open-door posture has turned into the bring-them-to-the-door policies of actively seeking to identify and encourage talented youngsters. California's state system comes close to bringing the doors to the students.

Is there any real issue of maintaining diversity in the state and city universities whose doors are kept as wide open as possible, sometimes aggressively so? As long as they are able to expand to take care of the demand for places, they achieved a genuine diversity which made the results of . . . the private colleges look pale. But as the number of students seeking a college education rose sharply during the last decade, some institutions had to raise entrance standards to control enrollment, and others began to expand or create branch systems.   Out-of-state students came under tighter selection procedures.   The effect of higher entrance standards on one hand, or of a duplication of institutions within a state system on the other, particularly when "pecking orders" among the different branches exist—as they inevitably do in our society—is to reduce the socio-economic range and the range of interests and career plans of the student bodies in the more selective institutions.   This would not necessarily happen if the criteria for selection were not the "objective" ones of test scores and grades.   But most public institutions have made the point that subjective admissions in any substantial number of cases would be undesirable or politically impossible.   Perhaps that ends the matter. . . . But if that is the case it seems certain that within ten years a number of public colleges and universities will have lost a great deal of their constructive diversity.[21]

Without much more knowledge of the relationship of student characteristics, the environment in which formal education takes place, and the performance of these students after graduation, it seems as if the effort to retain flexibility in student selection, financing, and placement in colleges represents extremely valuable insurance against uncertainty as to what the optimum patterns really are for our society.

T. R. McConnell, Chairman of the Center for the Study of Higher Education at the University of California, closes his book, *A General Pattern for American Public Higher Education,* with the following plea.

Until we understand students more fully and have clearer ideas about the college experiences which will be most fruitful for them, many will make false starts and find it necessary to change directions. In some instances this may mean changing from one curriculum to another in the same institution.   In a functionally differentiated system of public higher education in which some fields and levels of specialization are assigned to particular institutions, change of direction may mean transferring from one institution to another.   Within the present limits of our knowledge about the "fit" between students and institutions, it would be indefensible, even in a coordinated and differentiated system, to assign a student once and for all to a particular institution or a specific curriculum.   The system must be flexible enough to enable each student to reach the highest level for which his aptitude and performance qualify him.[22]

This kind of flexibility, Dael Wolfle points out, has important positive benefits of its own.

Sizable portions of most professional groups have entered their professions after obtaining an undergraduate degree in some other field. From the standpoint of an individual, this situation may seem inefficient and to represent lost time; he started out to be one thing, changed his mind, and ended up something else. But from the standpoint of the professions themselves, there are advantages. Each professional group includes some members who are reasonably well acquainted with other fields. There are lawyers who know science. There are scientists who know economics, economists who know mathematics, and so on throughout the entire range of possible combinations. Collectively, each field includes a breadth of knowledge which it would not have if a student's occupational opportunities were restricted to the field in which he majored in college.[23]

.   .   .

Whether the career choice is made before or after leaving college, the graduate usually remains in his chosen field of work throughout the rest of his career. But even that is far from universal. Many liberal arts graduates and reasonable numbers of professional school graduates shift from one kind of work to another as their interests change and opportunities permit. The large amount of shifting which has gone on in the past has constituted an important method of adjusting the supply of educated workers to changing occupational demands. The existence of a sizable body of educated workers, flexible enough in skill and interest to move into fields in which the demands and rewards are greatest is a major national asset.[24]

The plea to preserve and encourage flexibility in the mechanisms by which many kinds of students distribute themselves throughout many kinds of colleges and throughout the full range of academic disciplines within these colleges is central to the main arguments of this book: it arises after watching a series of unexpectedly great pressures at work in student admissions and in college budgeting. Important elements of flexibility seem in danger of being withdrawn from our system of higher education. Perhaps there is still time to recognize these pressures and somehow to change the direction in which they are urging us.

Notes

[1] U.S. Office of Education, *Projections of Educational Statistics to 1973–74* (Washington, D.C.: U.S. Government Printing Office, 1964); U.S. Office of Education, News Release HEW-121 dated December 28, 1965.

[2] John F. Morse, "The Impact of Government Programs on Student Aid Administration," in *Student Financial Aid and Institutional Purpose* (New York: College Entrance Examination Board, 1963), p. 6.

[3] See Allan M. Cartter and Robert Farrell, "Higher Education in the Last Third of the Century," *Educational Record*, Vol. 46, No. 2 (Spring 1965), pp. 119–128; Allan M. Cartter, "A New Look at the Supply of College Teachers," *Educational Record*, Vol. 46, No. 3 (Summer 1965), pp. 267–277; Ray C. Maul, *Teacher Supply and Demand in Universities, Colleges, and Junior Colleges, 1961–62 and 1962–63*, Research Report 1963 (Washington, D.C.: National Education Association, 1963); Daniel Patrick Moynihan, "The Impact on Manpower Development and Employment of Youth," in Earl J. McGrath (ed.), *Universal Higher Education, op. cit.*, pp. 65–103; Seymour E. Harris, "Financing of Higher Education: Broad Issues," in Dexter M. Keezer (ed.), *Financing Higher Education: 1960–1970, op. cit.*, pp. 35–78.

[4] Frank H. Bowles, *Access to Higher Education*, Vol. I, *op. cit.*, pp. 158–159.

[5] *Ibid.*, pp. 159, 160.

[6] The concern, however, for making available second chances is not uniquely American. The Report of the Robbins Commmittee in Great Britain (Chapter II, "Aims and Principles," p. 9) is but one example:

> If it is true that certain differences of level and function must be expected to persist among institutions, it is also true that such a structure can only be morally acceptable if there are opportunities for the transfer of a student from one institution to another when this is appropriate to his or her intellectual attainments and educational needs. We attach great importance to this.

[7] Dael Wolfle, *America's Resources of Specialized Talent* (New York: Harper and Bros., 1954), pp. 143, 146, and 152; Daniel Patrick Moynihan, "The Impact on Manpower Development and Employment of Youth," in Earl J. McGrath (ed.), *Universal Higher Education, op. cit.*, p. 81. The aptitude tests used and sampling methods differed in these two estimates, and hence may not be strictly comparable.

[8] Frank H. Bowles, *Access to Higher Education*, Vol. I, *op. cit.*, p. 162.

[9] Frank H. Bowles, "Contrasts in Education: Europe and the U.S.," *College Board Review*, Vol. 46 (Winter, 1962), pp. 13–18.

[10] Dr. J. Harold Goldthorpe, Bureau of Higher Education, U.S. Office of Education, provided this information. Published documentation through 1960–61 is found in his contribution to Chapter 12 of Seymour H. Harris (ed.), *Education and Public Policy* (Berkeley: McCutchan Publishing Corp., 1965).

[11] John F. Morse, "They Do Not Serve Who Only Stand and Wait," *Journal of the Association of College Admissions Counsellors*, Vol. IX, No. 3 (Winter 1964), p. 19.

[12] Bowles, "Contrasts in Education: Europe and the U.S.," *op. cit.*, p. 17.

[13] Lees, "Financing Higher Education in the United States and Britain," *op. cit.*, pp. 332–33.

[14] Bowen here is discussing the "social benefits" of higher education in the United States and Great Britain in a general and illustrative way. The conclusion that more university education automatically enriches a democratic society isn't necessarily so. If university education were, say, to become only an over-filled pipeline into government service, with the most successful students receiving the jobs they hoped for, and becoming entrenched bureaucrats, and the other students accepting inferior government jobs or choosing to become unemployed revolutionaries, one's judgment about expanding that form of higher education could well differ. This description, starkly drawn, unfortunately, does describe the situation in several nations.

[15] This last statement represents political-social judgment as well as economic theory. Some economists, proceeding from other judgments, argue that the social wisdom of large private donors is as good if not better than that of the voting public, and that therefore private donors should be counted upon as the major source of needed and non-student income in higher education. Other economists have argued that education is primarily a national responsibility, like defense, and is best financed solely through taxation and government spending. Both statements—and the ones which lie in between—are controversial, and properly so.

[16] William G. Bowen, "University Finance in Britain and the United States: Implications of Financing Arrangements for Educational Issues," *Public Finance,* Vol. XVIII, No. 1 (1963), pp. 55–58, 82–83.

[17] Milton Friedman, "The Role of Government in Education," in Robert A. Solo (ed.), *Economics and the Public Interest* (New Brunswick, N.J.: Rutgers University Press, 1955).

[18] John Vaizey, *The Economics of Education* (New York: Free Press of Glencoe, Inc., 1962), p. 32 ff.

[19] In theory it would be possible, and perhaps even generally desirable for some colleges to modify their apparently built-in ambitions to raise steadily the objective academic qualifications of their entering classes, and instead shift their major hospitality towards the middle-aptitude range, where the greatest new student demand seems most likely to develop if offered appropriate instruction. Thus far, however, the established institutions seem overwhelmingly to have avoided this choice, leaving the new demands to be met by new, usually public, institutions.

[20] André L. Danière, *Higher Education in the American Economy* (New York: Random House, 1964), p. 129.

[21] Reprinted with permission from Fred L. Glimp, "Student Diversity and National Goals in Higher Education," in College Scholarship Service, *The Economics of Higher Education* (New York: College Entrance Examination Board, 1967), pp. 19–20.

[22] T. R. McConnell, *A General Pattern for American Public Higher Education,* Carnegie Series in American Education (New York: McGraw-Hill Book Co., 1962), p. 190.

[23] Dael Wolfle, *America's Resources of Specialized Talent, op. cit.*, p. 74.

[24] *Ibid.*, p. 269.

A

Appendix: Joint Distribution Tables for Selected Years Projected through 1974-75

A GUIDE TO READING THE JOINT DISTRIBUTION TABLES

Family income in the tables

At each percentile level of family income, two supplementary figures are listed. The first figure represents the corresponding income for families where the head is between the ages of 35 and 64 (see the notes beginning on page 146); the second figure, in parentheses, represents an estimate by the College Scholarship Service of the amount of money a normal-budget, three-child family might be expected to contribute each year to a son's (or a daughter's) college education. The College Scholarship Service curves used for making these estimates are reproduced in Appendix B.

Reading the tables

Each table presents the number of high school graduates as described in the title according to scores on the College Entrance Examination Board Scholastic Aptitude Test (verbal section) *and* the annual income of their families.

Each cell in a table contains two estimates of the size of the national pool of high school graduates defined according to aptitude and income. The first estimate assumes a coefficient of correlation between aptitude and income of 0.4. This appears to be the most appropriate coefficient to use for these estimates. The second estimate is the result of a similar calculation, but a correlation coefficient of 0.7 is assumed.

TABLE

Joint distribution of U.S. male high school

SAT score		200	250	300	350
SAT percentile (adjusted)		0	14	31	46

Family income					
Percentile	Amount (Possible contribution)				
0	$000	648,000	555,000	450,000	347,000
	($000)	648,000	555,000	450,000	347,000
20	$2810	534,000	467,000	388,000	307,000
	($000)	538,000	479,000	414,000	331,000
40	$4340	407,000	362,000	306,000	249,000
	($250)	421,000	387,000	339,000	285,000
60	$5960	277,000	250,000	215,000	174,000
	($460)	285,000	267,000	242,000	215,000
80	$8230	140,000	129,000	114,000	98,000
	($860)	143,000	136,000	127,000	119,000
85	$10,350	105,000	97,000	86,000	81,000
	($1320)	107,000	101,000	95,000	91,000
90	$12,470	71,000	65,000	59,000	52,000
	($1900)	72,000	68,000	64,000	62,000
95	$14,600	36,000	33,000	30,000	27,000
	($2500)	36,000	34,000	33,000	32,000

A-1

graduates: aptitude and family income 1954–55

361	400	450	500	550	600	650
Mean	63	77	88	94	98	99

324,000	240,000	149,000	80,000	37,000	15,000	5000
324,000	240,000	149,000	80,000	37,000	15,000	5000
288,000	218,000	138,000	76,000	35,000	15,000	5000
310,000	234,000	147,000	80,000	37,000	15,000	5000
235,000	182,000	119,000	67,000	32,000	14,000	5000
271,000	216,000	139,000	77,000	37,000	15,000	5000
171,000	136,000	92,000	54,000	27,000	12,000	4000
207,000	171,000	119,000	70,000	35,000	15,000	5000
94,000	78,000	55,000	34,000	18,000	8000	3000
116,000	103,000	80,000	52,000	29,000	13,000	5000
72,000	59,000	43,000	27,000	15,000	7000	3000
89,000	81,000	65,000	44,000	25,000	12,000	5000
50,000	47,000	31,000	20,000	11,000	5000	2000
62,000	57,000	48,000	34,000	21,000	10,000	4000
27,000	23,000	18,000	12,000	7000	3000	1000
32,000	31,000	27,000	21,000	14,000	8000	3000

Total: 648,000

TABLE

Joint distribution of U.S. male high school

SAT score	200	250	300	350
SAT percentile (adjusted)	0	14	31	46

Family income

Percentile	Amount (Possible contribution)				
0	$000	898,000	769,000	623,000	481,000
	($000)	898,000	769,000	623,000	481,000
20	$3320	740,000	648,000	537,000	426,000
	($140)	746,000	664,000	574,000	458,000
40	$5200	564,000	502,000	424,000	349,000
	($350)	583,000	536,000	470,000	395,000
60	$7260	383,000	346,000	299,000	241,000
	($680)	395,000	370,000	335,000	297,000
80	$10,310	194,000	178,000	157,000	136,000
	($1310)	198,000	188,000	175,000	165,000
85	$13,000	145,000	134,000	119,000	112,000
	($2040)	148,000	140,000	132,000	126,000
90	$15,690	98,000	91,000	81,000	72,000
	($2900)	99,000	94,000	89,000	86,000
95	$18,389	50,000	46,000	42,000	38,000
	($3600)	50,000	48,000	46,000	45,000

A-2

graduates: aptitude and family income 1959–60

361	400	450	500	550	600	650
Mean	63	77	88	94	98	99

449,000	332,000	207,000	111,000	51,000	21,000	8000
449,000	332,000	207,000	111,000	51,000	21,000	8000
399,000	302,000	192,000	105,000	49,000	20,000	7000
430,000	325,000	204,000	110,000	45,000	21,000	8000
326,000	252,000	164,000	92,000	45,000	19,000	7000
375,000	295,000	193,000	107,000	51,000	21,000	8000
237,000	188,000	127,000	74,000	37,000	16,000	6000
287,000	237,000	166,000	98,000	48,000	20,000	7000
131,000	107,000	76,000	47,000	25,000	11,000	4000
161,000	143,000	111,000	73,000	40,000	18,000	7000
100,000	82,000	60,000	38,000	20,000	10,000	4000
124,000	112,000	90,000	61,000	35,000	17,000	6000
70,000	65,000	44,000	28,000	16,000	8000	3000
85,000	79,000	66,000	48,000	29,000	14,000	6000
37,000	32,000	24,000	16,000	9000	5000	2000
44,000	42,000	37,000	29,000	19,000	11,000	5000

Total: 898,000

TABLE

Joint distribution of U.S. male high school

SAT score		200	250	300	350
SAT percentile (adjusted)		0	14	31	46

Family income					
Percentile	Amount (Possible contribution)				
0	$000	941,000	806,000	653,000	504,000
	($000)	941,000	806,000	653,000	504,000
20	$3600	776,000	679,000	563,000	446,000
	($170)	781,000	696,000	601,000	430,000
40	$5600	591,000	526,000	445,000	361,000
	($400)	611,000	561,000	492,000	414,000
60	$7850	402,000	362,000	313,000	253,000
	($790)	413,000	387,000	351,000	312,000
80	$11,300	203,000	187,000	165,000	143,000
	($1580)	208,000	197,000	184,000	173,000
85	$14,000	152,000	140,000	125,000	118,000
	($2350)	155,000	147,000	138,000	132,000
90	$17,100	102,000	95,000	85,000	76,000
	($3380)	104,000	99,000	94,000	91,000
95	$20,000	52,000	49,000	44,000	40,000
	($4500)	53,000	50,000	48,000	47,000

A-3

graduates: aptitude and family income 1961–62

361	400	450	500	550	600	650
Mean 63	77	88	94	98	99	

471,000	348,000	216,000	116,000	54,000	22,000	8000
471,000	348,000	216,000	116,000	54,000	22,000	8000
418,000	317,000	201,000	110,000	51,000	21,000	7000
451,000	340,000	214,000	115,000	54,000	22,000	8000
341,000	264,000	172,000	97,000	47,000	20,000	7000
393,000	309,000	202,000	112,000	53,000	22,000	8000
248,000	197,000	133,000	78,000	39,000	17,000	6000
300,000	249,000	174,000	102,000	50,000	21,000	7000
137,000	113,000	80,000	49,000	26,000	12,000	5000
169,000	150,000	116,000	76,000	41,000	19,000	7000
105,000	86,000	63,000	40,000	21,000	10,000	4000
130,000	117,000	94,000	64,000	37,000	17,000	7000
73,000	68,000	46,000	29,000	16,000	8000	3000
89,000	83,000	69,000	50,000	30,000	15,000	6000
39,000	33,000	26,000	17,000	10,000	5000	2000
46,000	44,000	39,000	30,000	20,000	11,000	5000

Total: 941,000

TABLE

Joint distribution of U.S. male high school

SAT score		200	250	300	350
SAT percentile (adjusted)		0	14	31	46

Family income					
Percentile	Amount (Possible contribution)				
0	$000	1,129,000	967,000	783,000	604,000
	($000)	1,129,000	967,000	783,000	604,000
20	$3800	931,000	814,000	676,000	535,000
	($190)	937,000	835,000	721,000	576,000
40	$6050	709,000	632,000	534,000	434,000
	($480)	733,000	674,000	591,000	497,000
60	$8500	482,000	435,000	375,000	303,000
	($920)	496,000	465,000	422,000	374,000
80	$12,400	244,000	224,000	198,000	171,000
	($1880)	249,000	236,000	220,000	207,000
85	$15,300	182,000	168,000	150,000	141,000
	($2800)	186,000	176,000	166,000	158,000
90	$19,000	123,000	114,000	102,000	91,000
	($4100)	125,000	119,000	112,000	109,000
95	$22,000	62,000	58,000	53,000	48,000
	($5300)	63,000	60,000	57,000	56,000

A-4

graduates: aptitude and family income 1963–64

361	400	450	500	550	600	650
Mean	63	77	88	94	98	99

565,000	418,000	260,000	139,000	65,000	26,000	9000
565,000	418,000	260,000	139,000	65,000	26,000	9000
502,000	380,000	241,000	132,000	62,000	26,000	8000
541,000	408,000	257,000	139,000	64,000	26,000	9000
409,000	317,000	207,000	116,000	56,000	24,000	8000
472,000	370,000	242,000	135,000	64,000	26,000	9000
298,000	237,000	160,000	93,000	47,000	20,000	7000
360,000	298,000	208,000	123,000	61,000	26,000	9000
164,000	135,000	96,000	59,000	31,000	14,000	6000
203,000	180,000	139,000	91,000	50,000	23,000	8000
126,000	103,000	76,000	48,000	26,000	12,000	5000
155,000	141,000	113,000	77,000	44,000	21,000	8000
88,000	82,000	55,000	35,000	20,000	9000	4000
107,000	100,000	83,000	60,000	36,000	18,000	7000
47,000	40,000	31,000	20,000	12,000	6000	2000
55,000	53,000	47,000	37,000	24,000	13,000	6000

Total: 1,129,000

TABLE

Joint distribution of U.S. male high school graduates:

SAT score		200	250	300	350
SAT percentile (adjusted)		0	14	31	46
Family income					
Percentile	Amount (Possible contribution)				
0	$000	1,337,000	1,145,000	928,000	716,000
	($000)	1,337,000	1,145,000	928,000	716,000
20	$3900	1,102,000	965,000	800,000	634,000
	($200)	1,110,000	989,000	854,000	682,000
40	$6300	840,000	748,000	632,000	513,000
	($510)	868,000	798,000	700,000	588,000
60	$8800	571,000	515,000	445,000	359,000
	($970)	587,000	550,000	499,000	443,000
80	$13,000	289,000	265,000	234,000	203,000
	($2040)	295,000	280,000	261,000	246,000
85	$16,000	216,000	199,000	177,000	167,000
	($3000)	220,000	209,000	196,000	187,000
90	$20,000	146,000	135,000	121,000	108,000
	($4500)	148,000	141,000	133,000	129,000
95	$23,000	74,000	69,000	63,000	57,000
	($5600)	75,000	71,000	68,000	66,000

A-5

aptitude and family income 1964–65 (estimated)

361	400	450	500	550	600	650
Mean	63	77	88	94	98	99

669,000	495,000	308,000	165,000	76,000	31,000	11,000
669,000	495,000	308,000	165,000	76,000	31,000	11,000
595,000	450,000	285,000	156,000	73,000	30,000	11,000
640,000	484,000	304,000	164,000	76,000	31,000	11,000
485,000	375,000	245,000	138,000	67,000	28,000	10,000
559,000	439,000	287,000	160,000	75,000	31,000	11,000
353,000	280,000	189,000	110,000	55,000	24,000	9000
427,000	353,000	247,000	145,000	72,000	30,000	11,000
194,000	160,000	113,000	70,000	37,000	17,000	7000
240,000	213,000	165,000	108,000	59,000	27,000	10,000
149,000	122,000	90,000	56,000	30,000	14,000	6000
184,000	167,000	134,000	91,000	52,000	25,000	9000
104,000	97,000	65,000	42,000	23,000	11,000	5000
127,000	118,000	99,000	71,000	43,000	22,000	9000
55,000	48,000	36,000	24,000	14,000	7000	3000
65,000	63,000	56,000	43,000	29,000	16,000	7000

Total: 1,337,000 (Estimate)

TABLE

Joint distribution of U.S. male high school graduates:

SAT score	200	250	300	350
SAT percentile (adjusted)	0	14	31	46

Family income					
Percentile	Amount (Possible contribution)				
0	$000	1,334,000	1,143,000	926,000	714,000
	($000)	1,334,000	1,143,000	926,000	714,000
20	$4000	1,100,000	962,000	798,000	632,000
	($200)	1,108,000	987,000	852,000	680,000
40	$6500	838,000	746,000	630,000	512,000
	($550)	866,000	796,000	698,000	587,000
60	$9500	569,000	514,000	444,000	359,000
	($1150)	586,000	549,000	498,000	442,000
80	$13,500	288,000	265,000	234,000	202,000
	($2200)	294,000	279,000	261,000	245,000
85	$16,700	215,000	199,000	177,000	167,000
	($3260)	219,000	209,000	196,000	187,000
90	$21,000	145,000	135,000	121,000	108,000
	($4900)	147,000	140,000	133,000	128,000
95	$24,000	74,000	69,000	63,000	57,000
	($6000)	74,000	71,000	67,000	66,000

A-6

aptitude and family income 1965–66 (projected)

361	400	450	500	550	600	650
Mean	63	77	88	94	98	99

667,000	494,000	307,000	164,000	76,000	31,000	11,000
667,000	494,000	307,000	164,000	76,000	31,000	11,000
593,000	449,000	285,000	156,000	73,000	30,000	11,000
639,000	483,000	303,000	164,000	76,000	31,000	11,000
484,000	374,000	244,000	137,000	66,000	28,000	10,000
557,000	438,000	286,000	159,000	75,000	31,000	11,000
352,000	280,000	189,000	110,000	55,000	24,000	9000
426,000	352,000	246,000	145,000	72,000	30,000	11,000
194,000	160,000	113,000	70,000	37,000	17,000	7000
240,000	213,000	164,000	108,000	59,000	27,000	10,000
149,000	121,000	89,000	56,000	30,000	14,000	6000
184,000	166,000	133,000	90,000	52,000	25,000	9000
104,000	97,000	65,000	42,000	23,000	11,000	5000
127,000	118,000	98,000	71,000	43,000	21,000	9000
55,000	47,000	36,000	24,000	14,000	7000	3000
65,000	63,000	55,000	43,000	28,000	16,000	7000

Total: 1,334,000 (Projected)

TABLE

Joint distribution of U.S. male high school graduates:

SAT score		200	250	300	350
SAT percentile (adjusted)		0	14	31	46
Family income					
Percentile	Amount (Possible contribution)				
0	$000 ($000)	1,353,000 1,353,000	1,159,000 1,159,000	939,000 939,000	724,000 724,000
20	$4300 ($250)	1,116,000 1,123,000	976,000 1,001,000	810,000 865,000	641,000 690,000
40	$7000 ($630)	850,000 879,000	757,000 807,000	639,000 708,000	520,000 595,000
60	$9900 ($1220)	578,000 595,000	521,000 557,000	450,000 505,000	364,000 448,000
80	$14,800 ($2610)	293,000 298,000	268,000 283,000	237,000 264,000	205,000 249,000
85	$18,200 ($3800)	219,000 222,000	202,000 211,000	179,000 198,000	169,000 190,000
90	$23,000 ($5600)	147,000 150,000	137,000 142,000	123,000 134,000	109,000 130,000
95	$26,200 ($6880)	75,000 75,000	70,000 72,000	63,000 68,000	57,000 67,000

A-7

aptitude and family income 1967–68 (projected)

361	400	450	500	550	600	650
Mean	63	77	88	94	98	99

677,000	501,000	312,000	167,000	77,000	32,000	11,000
677,000	501,000	312,000	167,000	77,000	32,000	11,000
602,000	455,000	289,000	158,000	74,000	31,000	11,000
648,000	489,000	308,000	166,000	77,000	32,000	11,000
491,000	380,000	248,000	139,000	67,000	28,000	10,000
565,000	444,000	290,000	161,000	76,000	31,000	11,000
357,000	284,000	192,000	112,000	56,000	24,000	9000
432,000	357,000	249,000	147,000	73,000	31,000	11,000
197,000	162,000	115,000	71,000	37,000	17,000	7000
243,000	216,000	167,000	110,000	60,000	27,000	10,000
151,000	123,000	91,000	57,000	31,000	14,000	6000
186,000	169,000	135,000	92,000	53,000	25,000	9000
105,000	98,000	67,000	42,000	23,000	11,000	5000
129,000	119,000	100,000	72,000	43,000	22,000	9000
56,000	48,000	37,000	24,000	14,000	7000	3000
66,000	64,000	56,000	44,000	29,000	16,000	7000

Total: 1,353,000 (Projected)

TABLE
Joint distribution of U.S. male high school graduates:

SAT score		200	250	300	350
SAT percentile (adjusted)		0	14	31	46

Family income					
Percentile	Amount (Possible contribution)				
0	$000	1,450,000	1,242,000	1,006,000	776,000
	($000)	1,450,000	1,242,000	1,006,000	776,000
20	$4600	1,196,000	1,046,000	868,000	687,000
	($270)	1,204,000	1,072,000	927,000	740,000
40	$7500	911,000	811,000	685,000	557,000
	($730)	942,000	865,000	759,000	638,000
60	$10,700	619,000	558,000	482,000	390,000
	($1420)	637,000	597,000	541,000	480,000
80	$16,200	313,000	288,000	254,000	220,000
	($3080)	320,000	303,000	283,000	266,000
85	$20,000	234,000	216,000	192,000	181,000
	($4500)	238,000	227,000	213,000	203,000
90	$25,300	158,000	146,000	132,000	117,000
	($6560)	160,000	153,000	144,000	140,000
95	$28,800	80,000	75,000	68,000	61,000
	($7920)	81,000	77,000	73,000	72,000

A-8

aptitude and family income 1969–70 (projected)

361	400	450	500	550	600	650
Mean	63	77	88	94	98	99

725,000	537,000	334,000	179,000	83,000	34,000	12,000
725,000	537,000	334,000	179,000	83,000	34,000	12,000
645,000	488,000	309,000	169,000	79,000	33,000	11,000
695,000	524,000	330,000	178,000	83,000	34,000	12,000
526,000	407,000	265,000	149,000	72,000	30,000	11,000
606,000	476,000	311,000	173,000	82,000	34,000	12,000
383,000	304,000	205,000	120,000	60,000	26,000	10,000
463,000	383,000	267,000	157,000	78,000	33,000	11,000
211,000	173,000	123,000	76,000	40,000	18,000	7000
261,000	231,000	179,000	117,000	64,000	29,000	11,000
162,000	132,000	97,000	61,000	33,000	16,000	6000
200,000	181,000	145,000	98,000	56,000	27,000	10,000
113,000	105,000	70,000	45,000	25,000	12,000	5000
138,000	128,000	107,000	77,000	47,000	23,000	9000
60,000	52,000	39,000	26,000	15,000	8000	3000
71,000	68,000	60,000	47,000	31,000	17,000	7000

Total: 1,450,000 (Projected)

TABLE

Joint distribution of U.S. male high school graduates

SAT score	200	250	300	350
SAT percentile (adjusted)	0	14	31	46

Family income					
Percentile	Amount (Possible contribution)				
0	$000	1,715,000	1,469,000	1,190,000	918,000
	($000)	1,715,000	1,469,000	1,190,000	918,000
20	$5400	1,414,000	1,237,000	1,026,000	813,000
	($390)	1,424,000	1,268,000	1,096,000	875,000
40	$9100	1,077,000	959,000	811,000	659,000
	($1040)	1,114,000	1,023,000	897,000	754,000
60	$12,900	732,000	661,000	570,000	461,000
	($2010)	754,000	706,000	640,000	568,000
80	$20,200	371,000	340,000	301,000	260,000
	($4580)	378,000	359,000	335,000	315,000
85	$24,700	260,000	256,000	227,000	215,000
	($6280)	282,000	268,000	252,000	240,000
90	$32,200	187,000	173,000	156,000	138,000
	($8880)	190,000	180,000	170,000	165,000
95	$35,800	95,000	88,000	80,000	73,000
	($10,320)	96,000	91,000	87,000	85,000

A-9

aptitude and family income 1974–75 (projected)

361	400	450	500	550	600	650
Mean	63	77	88	94	98	99

858,000	635,000	394,000	211,000	98,000	40,000	14,000
858,000	635,000	394,000	211,000	98,000	40,000	14,000
763,000	577,000	366,000	200,000	94,000	39,000	14,000
821,000	620,000	390,000	210,000	98,000	40,000	14,000
622,000	481,000	314,000	177,000	85,000	36,000	13,000
717,000	563,000	368,000	205,000	97,000	40,000	14,000
453,000	359,000	243,000	142,000	71,000	31,000	11,000
547,000	453,000	316,000	186,000	92,000	39,000	14,000
249,000	205,000	145,000	90,000	47,000	22,000	8000
308,000	273,000	211,000	139,000	75,000	34,000	13,000
192,000	156,000	115,000	72,000	39,000	18,000	7000
236,000	214,000	172,000	116,000	67,000	32,000	12,000
133,000	125,000	83,000	54,000	30,000	14,000	6000
163,000	151,000	126,000	91,000	55,000	28,000	11,000
71,000	61,000	46,000	31,000	18,000	9000	4000
84,000	81,000	71,000	56,000	37,000	20,000	9000

Total: 1,715,000 (Projected)

NOTES ON THE DERIVATION OF THE JOINT
DISTRIBUTION TABLES

If recent broad census enumerations or sample surveys were available to elicit accurate information both as to measured academic aptitude and as to family income for high school students or for graduates, then much of what follows would be unnecessary. Presented below is a summary of the sources, methods, and major assumptions used in constructing this series of joint distributions of measured academic aptitude and family income for U.S. male high school graduates when the separate pieces of the distributions had to be fitted together under less than the ideal circumstances. The general approach underlying this construction process has already been discussed in Chapter II. It should be noted below that where reasonable doubt exists as to the appropriate estimate or assumption to use in making calculations, care has been taken, first, to try to use the best approximation available, but also to try to make the errors of estimation and assumption occur, if anything, on the conservative side: "conservative" here meaning selecting assumed values least favorable to the main argument of the thesis, that is, tending to overstate rather than understate the size of the pools of students in the top half of the distributions of measured aptitude and family income. (The major finding of the study has been that the number of high school graduates who both score high on aptitude tests and come from prosperous families is much smaller than is generally thought to be the case.)

In order further to underscore the approximate nature of the calculations (beyond the clear warnings in Chapter II) each cell in the joint distribution tables in Appendix A presents a range of pool sizes, rather than a single estimate; the range runs from a conservative best estimate to the maximum plausible size.

Four major kinds of information are used to build the joint distribution tables in Appendix A: a distribution of measured aptitude, distributions of family income, estimates of the amount of money a normal-budget, three-child family might be expected (at different income levels) to contribute towards one child's annual college expenses, and enumerations or projections of the total number of U.S. male high school students who graduate each year:

1. Measured Aptitude.

   The 1960 survey of performance of high school seniors on the College Entrance Examination Board Preliminary Scholastic Aptitude Test, performed by Dean Siebel and others for Educational Testing Service, represents the basis for estimating the percentage of male high school graduates from 1955 to 1975 likely to equal or exceed given score levels.   A distribution of SAT scores for male and female high school seniors, also based upon the Siebel study, is found in *College Board Score Reports* (Princeton, N.J., College Entrance Examination Board, 1963), Table 7, p. 18.

2. Family Income.

   A distribution of family incomes, by age of family head, is given in U.S. Bureau of the Census, *Trends in the Income of Families and Persons in the United States: 1947 to 1960*, Technical Paper No. 8 (U.S. Government Printing Office, Washington, D.C., 1963). Since family income is higher for families whose head is of an age most likely to have college-age children, an upward adjustment from the mean figures at each percentile level seemed desirable.

   However, the Census Population Surveys above in other ways seem less desirable for the purpose of this study than the family income surveys produced by the Office of Business Economics (OBE). The OBE surveys use a more comprehensive definition of family income, a definition which places more families in higher income brackets.   The CPS surveys recently have obtained "about 87 percent of the comparable total money income aggregates and about 94 percent of the comparable money wage or salary aggregates included in the personal income series prepared by the OBE." [1]

   The OBE definition of personal income represents "the current income received by families and unattached individuals from all sources, including wage and salary receipts (not of social insurance contributions), other labor income, proprietors' and rental income, dividends, personal interest income, and transfer payments.   In addition to monetary income flows (and in contrast with the CPS figures) personal income includes certain non-money items such as wages in kind, the value of food and fuel produced and consumed on farms, the net imputed rental value of owner-occupied homes, and imputed interest." [2]

Since it seemed desirable to use the basic OBE family income distribution, but also to adjust it for age of family head, the following adjustment method was used.

$$\frac{\text{CPS grand mean}}{\text{OBE grand mean}} = \frac{\text{CPS weighted mean (family heads 35–64)}}{\text{OBE weighted mean (family heads 35–64)}}$$

Three terms of the equation are known; the denominator of the right hand side is not. The CPS figures are found on page 75 of *Trends in the Income of Families and Persons in the United States;* the OBE figure comes from Jeannette M. Fitzwilliams, "Size Distribution of Income in 1963," *Survey of Current Business,* Office of Business Economics, U.S. Department of Commerce, Vol. 44, No. 4 (April 1964), Table 10. In weighting the CPS figures the age brackets 35–44 and 55–64 were assigned a weight of 1; 45–54 was assigned a weight of 2.

Before completing this operation for all the income percentile levels included in each of the selected years for Appendix A, it was necessary by linear interpolation to calculate CPS figures for 85th and 90th percentile levels, which are not given in the standard tables but which seemed of interest to this study.

The calculated OBE weighted family income figures correspond to the income percentile levels in Appendix A (20th, 40th, 60th, 80th, 85th, 90th and 95th percentiles). Using the rate of increase established in the OBE weighted means from 1955 to 1960, weighted means were projected to 1975. Income levels calculated are in current dollars.

One check on the validity of the adjustment of the CPS figures to the higher OBE levels comes from the 1/1000th Sample Survey data in the 1960 U.S. Census. The Sample Survey, available on computer tapes from the U.S. Bureau of the Census, provides individual questionnaire records for families surveyed. It was thus possible to select the family record of each family associated with each 17-year-old enumerated. From this selection, it was possible to obtain a 1960 family income distribution for the families of 17-year-olds enrolled in secondary schools. At every percentile level in the table calculated above, the family incomes from the 1960 Census 1/1000th survey were within $400 of the family incomes calculated by the adjustment method used in the present study. Unfortunately this kind of verification is available only for the 1960 Census year; the results of that inquiry, however, add some confidence one may place in the adjustment methods used here for the continuing series of CPS and OBE family income figures.

3. Estimate of the amount a normal-budget, three-child family can afford to contribute towards one child's annual college expenses.

For each income level, assuming a normal-budget situation, the College Scholarship Service provides tables and charts which suggest the contribution a family might reasonably be expected to contribute to a child's education. If the son who is to attend college neither works, borrows, or receives a scholarship (or draws down his own savings), this contribution figure must equal the full-cost student budget figure. To the extent a student is able to help himself, or is aided by scholarship, this constraint is relaxed. The CSS expectations were originally worked out after analyzing what parents had been willing to offer; college scholarship stipends in colleges using the CSS estimating procedures since 1954 have used these expected family contributions as an input to setting individual scholarship stipends and loan limits. The CSS chart for family expected contributions in normal-budget situations is reproduced as Appendix B. Family contributions for income levels in excess of $20,000 were estimated by extrapolation of the three-child curve. A 1967 revision to the CSS charts, which estimates somewhat smaller family contributions in the $10,000–$20,000 income brackets, has not been incorporated into this study.

4. Number of Male High School Graduates.

Enrollments since 1955 and all projections are from U.S. Office of Education, *Projections of Educational Statistics to 1974–75* (Washington: U.S. Government Printing Office, 1965), Table 14.

PRINCIPLES OF COMPUTATION

If one can assume that two related variables are jointly normally distributed, it is possible to determine joint frequencies in specified cells by reference to (a) the coefficient of correlation and the total population, if cell limits are specified in terms of normal Z-scores or percentile limits within the marginal distributions, or (b) the coefficient of correlation and the marginal distributions, if cell limits are specified in terms of the original scores.[3] Karl Pearson's *Tables for Statisticians and Biometricians* (first edition), Part II, Tables VIII and IX (*Volumes of Normal Bivariate Surfaces, Positive and Negative Correlation*), provide cell probabilities associated with Z-scores of 0.0 to 2.6 for both variables, using coefficients of correlation from −1.0 to +1.0.

It is clear that our two variables do not follow precisely the joint normal bivariate distribution. If they did, the marginal distributions would themselves be normal. But the comparisons which follow show that they are not normal. The comparisons also disclose that normality is reasonably well approximated by the SAT distribution, as well as by the upper portion of the income distribution (which is the range of greatest interest for this study). The closeness to normality of the marginal distributions in the portions of greatest interest to us is sufficient so that one can reasonably expect the joint distribution of *normalized* aptitude and *normalized* income to be close to a bivariate normal distribution in the relevant area, and this assumption was followed. Rather than first normalizing and then translating back into the original variables, the procedure was as follows:

1. To compute bivariate normal cell probabilities from the Pearson tables, having specified cell limits in terms of percentiles of the marginal distributions.
   (Note that these cell probabilities are cumulative; that is, they represent the probability of occurrence for levels at, or higher than the marginal percentile levels designated.)
2. To multiply cell probabilities times total population to obtain estimates of cell populations (which, again, are cumulative).
3. To translate the percentile levels of the marginal distributions into absolute levels of aptitude test scores and family annual dollar incomes by reference to the corresponding percentile limits of the actual distributions.

COMPARISON BETWEEN ACTUAL DISTRIBUTIONS AND NORMALITY

The College Board SAT score distribution approximates, but is not precisely, a normal distribution. How much this fact owes to sampling error in the SAT distribution, and how much to actual skewness in the total population distribution, is not known. Table A-10 following compares, for each SAT score level in the Appendix A tables, the calculated percentile level produced by the College Board with the percentile level produced by the

TABLE A-10

Percentile levels for male high school graduates represented by selected verbal SAT scores, from CEEB calculations, under assumption of normality, and after adjustment for common zero-point *

Verbal SAT score	(1) CEEB calculates this percentile level	(2) Assumption of normality generates this percentile level	(3) Difference between CEEB (1) and normal assumption	(4) Column 2 adjusted for equality of V200 with zero percentile level	(5) Difference between Columns 1 and 4
200	3	9	−6	0	+3
250	12	18	−6	14	−2
300	32	31	+1	31	+1
350	50	46	+4	46	+4
361	—	Adjusted mean $[(350 + 372) \div 2]$			
372	Mean	—			
400	65	63	+2	63	+2
450	76	77	−1	77	−1
500	85	88	−3	88	−3
550	91	94	−3	94	−3
600	97	98	−1	98	−1
650	99	99	0	99	0

*CEEB calculations are taken from *College Board Score Reports* (Princeton, N.J.: College Entrance Examination Board, 1963), Table 7, p. 18. The normal distribution in Column 2 is defined by an adjusted mean, derived by taking the average of the mean and the median of the CEEB distribution and a standard deviation of 120. In making the final adjustment, each of the probabilities at the V200 level were multiplied by an adjustment factor of 1.10036; each of the probabilities at the V250 level were multiplied by an adjustment factor of 1.05018.

assumption of normality. Since neither calculation produced a distribution where a SAT verbal score of 200, the minimum possible score on the SAT scale, represented the zero percentile level in the population, a second adjustment was made for the V200 and V250 percentile levels of aptitude. With this second adjustment, all U.S. male high school graduates are distributed at, or above the minimum possible verbal SAT score.

The distribution of U.S. family incomes is a skewed distribution. The distribution of family income where the age of the head of the family is 45–54 (the most heavily weighted age group, as described above), and 35–44 and 55–64, while less skewed, still are not normal. The nonnormality, however, particularly in the upper half of the distribution, does not seem so great as to invalidate its use with the Pearson tables for estimating the ranges of cell values in Appendix A. The following table illustrates the difference between the percentage of U.S.

TABLE A-11

Percentage of U.S. families (head aged 45–54) in each census income category, 1960, actual and predicted under assumption of normality.*

Income class (1959 dollars)	Percentage of families (actual)	Percentage of families (predicted)	Difference between actual and normal prediction
Less than $1000	8.5	3.7	4.8
$1000–$1999	5.1	4.2	0.9
$2000–$2999	6.1	6.0	0.1
$3000–$3999	7.7	7.1	0.6
$4000–$4999	9.4	8.0	1.4
$5000–$5999	11.5	8.6	2.9
$6000–$6999	10.1	8.8	1.3
$7000–$9999	23.3	23.7	− 0.4
$10,000 and over	18.3	29.9	−11.6

* The actual income distribution is from Herman P. Miller, *Trends in the Income of Families and Persons in the United States: 1947 to 1960, op. cit.,* p. 200. The predicted distribution under the assumption of normality was calculated here using a mean of $6500 and a standard deviation of $4500.

families (head age 45–54) in 1960 enumerated in each Census income category, and the percentage one might predict under the assumption of normality in the distribution.

Note in the summary table that the assumption of normality places a higher number of families in the top income class than does the actual distribution; for this high-income portion of the distribution, the assumption of normality tends to overstate the number of U.S. male high school graduates (in the Appendix A tables) who come from the most prosperous families. The direction of discrepancy thus tends to be conservative as it relates to the main findings of the study.

RANGE OF CORRELATION ESTIMATES

Ideally, one would prefer to operate with probability estimates of the correlation coefficient and to obtain corresponding probability estimates of frequencies in the cells. In this instance, unfortunately, the most that can be provided is a range of alternative estimates. It seems likely, however, that the probability of the actual correlation coefficient exceeding the upper limit of the estimated range is small. The general considerations involved have already been discussed briefly in Chapter II. Family income has been demonstrated to be positively related to indices of socioeconomic status, and by some definitions is explicitly included as one of its components. Both family income and family socioeconomic status have consistently been demonstrated to have positive correlation with the measured academic aptitude of offspring, particularly as the age of the offspring moves into the teen years. Summaries of the literature on the correlation between socioeconomic status and intelligence test scores, made by Neff, Miner, Anastasi, and Charters and Gage indicate that the correlations most frequently are in the range between 0.2 to 0.5, with the predominant results in the range of 0.35 to 0.4.[4]

Unfortunately, no large and representative sample study has been conducted which has determined reliably for the U.S. high school student population the degree of correlation between student measured aptitude and family income. Project TALENT in 1960 did collect aptitude and family income data from roughly 400,000 ninth-, tenth-, eleventh-, and twelfth-grade students, but the income information was elicited from student estimates in broad income categories, and was later considered insufficiently reliable to warrant an attempt at correlation with the student aptitude test score results.[5]

In this present study, an initial selection of 0.4 was made from among the plausible range of choices suggested by the literature previously noted. While chosen as a best estimate, it also seemed to be a conservative choice for the purposes of this study: that is, of the most plausible choices it was the highest one, and thus the one which, when worked through the Pearson tables, would produce the highest cell probabilities for high percentile levels of measured aptitude and of family income.

This choice was then tested against the only large sample of empirical, external data available: the National Merit semifinalist test scores and family income data described in detail in Chapter II. By using the procedures described above and entering the Pearson tables with a coefficient of correlation of 0.4, the joint distribution method derived here produced a pool of U.S. high school graduates estimated to be able to score the equivalent of 636 or better on the SAT and coming from families earning $15,000 or more numbering 7500 students. National Merit, which tested most (but not all) of the male high school seniors at this ability level and above, reported counting 5000 students in 1964 as being this able and prosperous, and, allowing for incomplete coverage of their testing program, further estimated that the total group probably numbered between 5500 and 6000. At this particular level of family income and measured aptitude, the predicted results and the actual results emerge relatively close together, with the predicted value erring on the side of conservatism (tending to overstate the size of the pool thus defined).

While the coefficient of correlation of 0.4 has been used throughout the study as representing a conservative best estimate, the results obtained thereby were surprising enough and the methods of obtaining the results were indirect and approximate enough so that it seemed unwise to imply in any way that a single set of reliable estimates had been achieved. Therefore a second set of calculations was made, using a coefficient of correlation of 0.7—the highest one conceivable (and perhaps then some). Each cell in the tables of Appendix A thus gives two estimates which form a range of estimate between the conservative best-guess and the probable maximum figure. Most of the main arguments remain undamaged even when skeptics choose to substitute the latter figure for the former in each of the examples cited in the text.

One may also legitimately inquire whether the estimated degree of relationship between the two variables actually does hold constant throughout the full range of their distributions, which is an implicit assumption in the mathematical construction of the Pearson bivariate distribution tables. Unfortunately, direct evidence is again lacking. The National Merit data suggests that, in the high-aptitude, high-income portion of the joint distribution, a coefficient of correlation of 0.4 is not unreasonable; but this information of itself seems insufficient to either prove or disprove this last question.

Notes

[1] U.S. Bureau of the Census, *Trends in the Income of Families and Persons in the United States; 1947 to 1960*, Technical Paper No. 8, U.S. Government Printing Office, Washington, D.C., 1963, p. 31.

[2] Selma F. Goldsmith, "Size Distribution of Personal Income," *Survey of Current Business*, Office of Business Economics, U.S. Department of Commerce, Vol. 38, No. 4, April 1958, p. 14.

[3] Karl Pearson, *Tables for Statisticians and Biometricians, First Edition, Part II, op. cit.*, p. lii.

[4] W. S. Neff, "Socioeconomic Status and Intelligence; A Critical Survey," *Psychological Bulletin*, 1938, Vol. 35, pp. 727–757, quoted in John B. Miner, *Intelligence in the United States* (New York: Springer Publishing Co., 1957), pp. 78–84; Anne Anastasi, *Differential Psychology*, third edition (New York: Macmillan Co., 1959), Chapter 15; and W. W. Charters, Jr., and N. L. Gage, *op. cit.*, pp. 12–21.

[5] John C. Flanagan and William W. Cooley, *Project TALENT: One-Year Follow-up Studies*, Cooperative Research Project Number 2333, Pittsburgh: University of Pittsburgh School of Education, 1966, p. 1; telephone conversations with William W. Cooley January 6, 1966 and January 24, 1967.

B

Appendix: College Scholarship Service Expected Contribution for College Expenses

CHART I °

CSS expectation from parents' net income for cases with no allowances and with Standard Federal Income Tax Deductions †

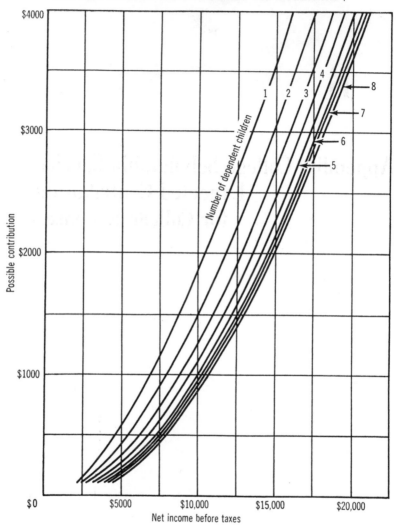

* This chart shows, in graphic form, approximately how much CSS expects families to provide from income each year for the college expenses of a child, *providing* the family claims the standard deduction for federal income tax purposes, and *providing* there are no special allowances which should be granted under CSS procedures.

† Reprinted with permission from the *1964–65 Supplement to Financial Aid Manual: 1962–64 Edition,* published in 1964 by the College Entrance Examination Board, New York.

C

Appendix: Changes in Student Budgets
and Minimum Effective SATs
for Six Groups of Colleges, 1962–64

TABLE C-1

Change in student expense budgets and minimum effective (10th percentile) Scholastic Aptitude Test (verbal) score levels for enrolled freshmen in six groups of colleges: 1962–64

Seven selective private universities	Total student expense for one resident year		Percentage of students receiving financial aid	Scholastic Aptitude Test verbal score for 10th percentile level of enrolled entering class	
	1962	*1964*	*1964*	*1962*	*1964*
Cornell University °	$3025	$3225	33	555 †	560 †
Dartmouth College	2900	3000	40	552	572
Duke University	2200	2400	40	460 †	520 †
Univ. of Pennsylvania	3050	3050	40	475	500
Princeton University	3060	3080	40	558	569
Stanford University	2685	2940	35	522 †	541 †
Yale University	3000	3000	40	547	585
Mean:	$2845	$2960	Mean: 524		550
Change:	+$115		Change: +26		
Eight selective private liberal arts colleges					
Amherst College	$2585	$2860	40	520	575
Bowdoin College	2505	2843	35	504	501
Carleton College	2500	2800	50	542 †	562 †
Pomona College	2830	2905	40	509 †	554 †
Reed College	2300	2600	35	587 †	590 †
Trinity College (Hartford, Ct.)	2725	2950	30	504	508
Wesleyan University	2650	2950	35	512	509
Williams College	2580	2700	30	582	538
Mean:	$2585	$2825	Mean: 532		542
Change:	+$240		Change +10		

° College of Arts and Sciences only.
† Scores here are for men only.

TABLE C-2

Change in student expense budgets and minimum effective (10th percentile) Scholastic Aptitude Test (verbal) score levels for enrolled freshmen in six groups of colleges: 1962–64 (cont.)

Six selective eastern women's colleges	Total student expense for one resident year		Percentage of students receiving financial aid	Scholastic Aptitude Test verbal score for 10th percentile level of enrolled entering class	
	1962	1964	1964	1962	1964
Bryn Mawr College	$2950	$3250	30	614	620
Mount Holyoke College	2900	3150	20	572	563
Radcliffe College	3025	3040	25	651	629
Smith College	3072	3072	25	558	579
Vassar College	3050	3350	20	552	561
Wellesley College	2900	2900	20	601	604
Mean:	$2985	$3125	Mean:	591	593
Change:	+$140		Change:	+2	
Seven small midwest private colleges					
Beloit College	$2575	$2775	35	425 *	473 *
Coe College	2190	2435	35	410 *	406 *
DePauw University	2300	2570	35	402 *	424 *
Denison University	2600	2700	35	461 *	462 *
Lake Forest College	2400	2800	25	428	455
Ohio Wesleyan University	2350	2600	35	472 *	455 *
Rockford College	2170	2300	45	406 *	454 *
Mean:	$2370	$2595	Mean:	430	447
Change:	+$225		Change:	+17	

* Scores here are for men only.

TABLE C-3

Change in student expense budgets and minimum effective (10th percentile) Scholastic Aptitude Test (verbal) score levels for enrolled freshmen in six groups of colleges: 1962–64

Six engineering colleges	Total student expense for one resident year		Percentage of students receiving financial aid	Scholastic Aptitude Test verbal score for 10th percentile level of enrolled class	
	1962	1964	1964	1962	1964
California Institute of Technology	$2600	$2900	60	579	600
Carnegie Institute of Technology	2585	3000	25	473	472
Case Institute of Technology	2786	2870	30	473	568
Massachusetts Institute of Technology	3056	3255	50	570	575
Rensselaer Polytechnic Institute	2763	2998	35	444	495
Worcester Polytechnic Institute	2670	2750	20	452	457
Mean:	$2745	$2955	Mean:	498	528
Change:	+$210		Change:	+30	
Five public universities					
University of Oregon	$1665 °	$1910 °	NR ‡	365 †	366 †
University of Virginia	2050 °	2200 °	30	428 †	466 †
University of Vermont	2275 °	2635 °	NR	401 §	404 §
University of Rhode Island	2220 °	2350 °	10	370 †	369 †
University of South Carolina	1530 °	1850 °	NR ‡	331 †	353 †
Mean:	$1950 °	$2190 °	Mean:	379	391
Change:	+$240		Change:	+12	

° In public university student budgets, the out-of-state student budget is

NOTES FOR APPENDIX C

Colleges and universities chosen for inclusion in Appendix C were selected partly to be representative of institutions with particular purposes or levels of entrance requirements, but only if they have provided comparable information to each of four different publications of the College Entrance Examination Board:
1. *The Manual of Freshman Class Profiles, 1962 Edition.*
2. *The Manual of Freshman Class Profiles, 1964 Edition.*
3. *The College Handbook, 1961–63.*
4. *The College Handbook, 1963–65.*

Obviously missing from listing among "selective private universities," due to nonreporting or noncomparable reporting, are, for example, Brown University, Columbia University, Harvard University, and the University of Chicago. Many of the public colleges and universities do not use College Board Tests for selection of students, and therefore are not represented in these publications.

The total student expense budgets for one resident year are listed in *The College Handbook.* Many of these budgets do not include estimates of personal expenses (travel, laundry, clothing, entertainment, etc.); in order to put all budgets on a comparable basis, an allowance of $400 per year has been made for personal expenses where these have not been otherwise estimated. The mean values in each subgroup in Appendix C were rounded to the nearest $5.

Some of the estimated percentages of students receiving financial aid come from *The College Handbook,* and others from the *Manuals of Freshman Class Profiles.* They are illustrative of general magnitude but not comparable in any exact sense.

In tabulating Scholastic Aptitude Test levels achieved, the

---

listed here. Cost for residents of the state where the public university is located is usually $300–500 less than the budget reported in this table. Also, commuting students pay $600–900 less to these universities for room and board, although they may face other costs of daily transportation and of living at home.

† Scores here are for men only.

‡ NR = not reported.

§ Scores here are for out-of-state men only.

10th percentile level was selected as more likely to represent an effective minimum pool boundary point than the lowest-score man enrolled.   Strictly speaking, the lowest-score man defines the selection pool, but in most colleges the percentage of students actually selected is low enough in the bottom tenth of the admitted score range so that its use in defining operating minima seems misleading.   Test score distribution patterns for entering classes are given in the *Manuals of Freshman Class Profiles*, with numbers of enrollees given in each 50-point segment.   Within these 50-point segments linear interpolation was used to estimate 10th percentile score levels.   With the exception of the women's colleges, and other colleges specifically noted in the tables, SAT scores are men's scores.

D

Appendix: The Distribution of Male Negro High School Graduates: 1964–65

The general approach to the construction of this kind of joint distribution is described in Chapter II and also in the notes for Appendix A. The different data sources, and treatment of data for the joint distribution of U.S. male Negro high school graduates for 1964–65 are described below.

1. Percentage able to equal or exceed given score levels on the verbal section of the SAT

On July 2, 1966, the U.S. Office of Education published *Equality of Educational Opportunity* (Washington: U.S. Government Printing Office, 1966), which included test results from a battery of five tests (nonverbal, verbal, reading, mathematics, and general information) administered by Educational Testing Service during the fall of 1965 to more than 191,000 12th grade students in 689 secondary schools and including about 50,000 nonwhite students. Henry S. Dyer, Vice President of Educational Testing Service, estimated that even though the verbal test results from this survey are not precisely comparable to the SAT verbal score norms used in Appendix A, they nonetheless were both sufficiently comparable to use in making rough estimates, and are at present the only national data for the verbal aptitude of twelfth-grade students, classified by ethnic background.

Here, the total population twelfth-grade verbal scores from the survey and the Negro scores were converted to the SAT scale. The survey verbal score means and standard deviations were 50 and 10, respectively for the total population, and 40.9 and 8.24 for the Negro students. Score results were not segregated by sex; these calculations have assumed male and female Negro score distributions to be the same. There are probably slight differences (tending to overstate the pool size for men and understate it for women at given score levels), but they are not likely serious ones. Dr. Robert C. Nichols, Research Director for the National Merit Scholarship Corporation, also reported that the National Achievement Scholarship Program conducted for Negro students by National Merit) in 1965 tested 3000 (out of a roughly estimated 3500 total in the nation) Negro seniors who were able to score 102 or better, which he estimated to be the rough equivalent of 500 or better on the verbal section of the SAT. Using the one-cell national estimate provided by Nichols, the U.S. Office of Education survey results were tested, yielding an initially estimated pool size for all income levels, at SAT 500 or better, of only about 1200 students. Since both the National Merit estimates and the USOE data results yielded smaller estimates than one might have anticipated, the choice was made to redefine the curve (assuming the curve to be a workable approximation of a normal curve), using the mean levels from the USOE survey, but a standard deviation derived from the USOE mean (40.9) and the National Merit experience: this yielded a new standard deviation of 9.19 which was used in these calculations, and which produces larger cell estimates in the high-aptitude range than would have been produced using only the USOE data. It is possible to imagine that, at the high- and low-score extremes of the distribution, the pool-size estimates may be in error by as much as 50 to 80 percent. Even so, the questions raised in Chapter II take account of this possibility, and the results still seem startling.

2. Family incomes that equal or exceed given amounts

The basic data for the income distribution used here are derived from the $\frac{1}{1000}$th Sample Survey tapes provided by the

U.S. Bureau of the Census from the 1960 Census. The tapes yield 2622 17-year-olds whose associated family records are also available for analysis. Of these, 265 17-year-olds were Negroes, and 255 were enumerated as part of a family where the head was either a parent or grandparent (and hence whose income source could be considered comparable for these purposes). Of these, in turn, 165 had completed more than tenth grade, as follows: 3 were enrolled in college, 12 were high school graduates but not enrolled in school or college, 41 were enrolled in twelfth grade and 109 in eleventh grade. Although for this selected age level the incomes of families of twelfth graders

TABLE D-1

Family incomes for Negro 17-year-olds, 1960, identified as college students, high school graduates not enrolled in further education, twelfth graders, or eleventh graders °

	Number of families in each income category distributed by enrollment category of associated 17-year-old				
Family income	12th grade enrolled	11th grade enrolled	college enrolled	high school graduate not enrolled	Total
Less than $1000	3	26			29
$1000–$1999	5	14		2	21
$2000–$2999	4	23		2	29
$3000–$3999	6	12		2	20
$4000–$4999	5	12			17
$5000–$5999	7	11		2	20
$6000–$6999	5	6	1	1	13
$7000–$7999		1		3	4
$8000–$9999	5	2	1		8
$10,000–$14,999	1	2			3
$15,000–$24,999			1		1
$25,000 and over					
Totals	41	109	3	12	165

° U.S. Census, ¹⁄₁₀₀₀th Sample Survey.

was slightly higher than for those of eleventh graders (these were the two largest groups in the sample), the four groups were combined. The basic distribution is provided above.

Family incomes were calculated for the 20th, 40th, 60th, 80th, and 95th percentile levels for 1960, and adjusted upwards to 1965 estimated levels using the proportion by which total incomes at these percentile levels increased during that period.

3. Number of male Negro high school graduates

The statistics enumerating male and female high school graduates in the United States each year do not include enumerations by race. The number of male Negro U.S. high school graduates for 1964–65 was estimated by setting up the following assumed proportional relationship.

$$\frac{\text{U.S. male Negro enrolled twelfth-graders (1960)}}{\text{U.S. total male enrolled twelfth-graders (1960)}} = \frac{\text{U.S. male Negro high school graduates (1965)}}{\text{U.S. total male high school graduates (1965)}}$$

4. SAT-income correlations

Chapter II describes the method used for associating percentile levels for aptitude test scores and percentile levels of student family income. Thomas F. Pettigrew, Associate Professor of Social Relations at Harvard University and a member of the advisory committee for the U.S. Office of Education Survey cited above, believes that the sociological and psychological factors working against good test performance among low-income Negro families may be such that the coefficient of correlation between family income and measured aptitude for Negro students may be higher than the 0.4 estimate used for the larger population. It may be, he thinks, as high as 0.5 and 0.6, but probably not 0.7 or higher. Since there are no directly comparable studies to test this, it remains a reasonable, but untested estimate to be considered when using the table.

Bibliography

BOOKS

Bowles, Frank H. *Access to Higher Education,* Vol. I. Paris: UNESCO and the International Association of Universities, 1963.

Buros, Oscar K. (ed.) *The Sixth Mental Measurements Yearbook.* Highland Park, N.J.: Gryphon Press, 1965, pp. 974–996.

Cass, James, and Birnbaum, Max. *Comparative Guide to American Colleges, 1965 Edition.* New York: Harper and Row, 1965.

Charters, W. W., Jr., and Gage, N. L. "Social Class and Intelligence Tests," *Readings in the Social Psychology of Education.* Boston: Allyn and Bacon, 1963, pp. 12–21.

College Handbook, 1961–63. New York: College Entrance Examination Board, 1961.

College Handbook, 1963–65. New York: College Entrance Examination Board, 1963.

College Scholarship Service. *Financial Aid Manual: 1962–64 Edition.* Princeton, N.J.: College Entrance Examination Board, 1962.

———. *1964–65 Supplement to Financial Aid Manual: 1962–64 Edition.* Princeton, N.J.: College Entrance Examination Board, 1964.

Danière, André L. *Higher Education in the American Economy.* New York: Random House, 1964.

Harris, Seymour E. (ed.). *Education and Public Policy.* Berkeley, Calif.: McCutchan Publishing Corp., 1965.

————. *Higher Education in the United States: The Economic Problems*. Cambridge, Mass.: Harvard University Press, 1960.

————. *Higher Education: Resources and Finance*. New York: McGraw-Hill Book Co., 1962.

————, DEITCH, KENNETH M., and LEVENSOHN, ALAN (eds.). *Challenge and Change in American Education*. Berkeley, California: McCutchan Publishing Corp., 1965.

HAVIGHURST, ROBERT J. *American Higher Education in the 1960s*. Columbus, Ohio: Ohio State University Press, 1960.

HOLLINSHEAD, BYRON S. *Who Should Go to College?* New York: Columbia University Press, 1952.

KEEZER, DEXTER M. (ed.). *Financing Higher Education: 1960–1970*. New York: McGraw-Hill Book Co., 1959.

KNAPP, ROBERT H. *The Origins of American Humanistic Scholars*. Englewood, N.J.: Prentice-Hall, Inc., 1964.

———— and GREENBAUM, JOSEPH J. *The Younger American Scholar*. Chicago: University of Chicago Press, 1953.

LANDSBERG, HANS H., FISCHMAN, LEONARD L., and FISHER, JOSEPH L. *Resources in America's Future: Patterns of Requirements and Availabilities, 1960–2000*. Baltimore: The Johns Hopkins Press, 1963.

LINDEN, FABIAN (ed.). *Expenditure Patterns of the American Family*. New York: National Industrial Conference Board, 1965.

Manual of Freshman Class Profiles, 1962 Edition. New York: College Entrance Examination Board, 1962.

Manual of Freshman Class Profiles, 1964 Edition. New York: College Entrance Examination Board, 1964.

Manual of Freshman Class Profiles, 1965–67 Edition. New York: College Entrance Examination Board, 1965.

McCONNELL, T. R. *A General Pattern for American Public Higher Education*. Carnegie Series in American Education. New York: McGraw-Hill Book Co., 1962.

McGRATH, EARL J. *The Predominantly Negro Colleges and Universities in Transition*. New York: Teachers College Press, Teachers College, Columbia University, 1965.

———— (ed.). *Universal Higher Education*. New York: McGraw-Hill Book Co., 1966.

MUSHKIN, SELMA J. (ed.). *Economics of Higher Education.* U.S. Office of Education. Washington: U.S. Government Printing Office, 1962.

PEARSON, KARL. *Tables for Statisticians and Biometricians,* First Edition, Part II. London: Cambridge University Press, 1931.

PETTIGREW, THOMAS F. *A Profile of the Negro American.* Princeton, N.J.: D. Van Nostrand Company, Inc., 1964.

RIESMAN, DAVID. *Constraint and Variety in American Education.* The University Lectures in the Humanities. Lincoln, Nebraska: University of Nebraska, 1956.

—— and JENCKS, CHRISTOPHER. *The Academic Revolution.* New York: Doubleday, 1968.

RUDOLPH, FREDERICK. *The American College and University.* New York: Alfred A. Knopf, 1962.

SANFORD, NEVITT (ed.). *The American College: A Psychological and Social Interpretation of the Higher Learning.* New York: John Wiley & Sons, Inc., 1962.

Student Financial Aid and Institutional Purpose. A Colloquium on Financial Aid held by the College Scholarship Service of the College Entrance Examination Board. New York: College Entrance Examination Board, 1963.

Student Financial Aid and National Purpose. A Colloquium on Financial Aid held by the College Scholarship Service of the College Entrance Examination Board. New York: College Entrance Examination Board, 1962.

VAIZEY, JOHN. *The Economics of Education.* New York: Free Press of Glencoe, Inc., 1962.

WHITEHEAD, ALFRED NORTH. *The Aims of Education and Other Essays.* New York: MacMillan Co., 1929.

WOLFLE, DAEL. *America's Resources of Specialized Talent.* New York: Harper and Bros., 1954.

PUBLIC DOCUMENTS

Great Britain. Committee on Higher Education. *Higher Education: Report of the Committee Appointed by the Prime Minister under the Chairmanship of Lord Robbins, 1961–63.* London: Her Majesty's Stationery Office, 1963.

U.S. Bureau of the Census. *Historical Statistics of the United States, Colonial Times to 1957*. Washington: U.S. Government Printing Office, 1960.

————. *1960 Census of Population*, Vol. 26. Washington: U.S. Government Printing Office, 1962.

————. *1960 Census of Population and Housing: 1/1000, 1/10,000 —Two National Samples of the Population of the United States*. Washington: U.S. Government Printing Office, 1964.

————. *1960 Census of Population: 1/1000th Sample Survey*. Washington: U.S. Bureau of the Census, 1964. (Data available from the Department of Social Relations at Harvard.)

————. *Statistical Abstract of the United States: 1964*. Washington: U.S. Government Printing Office, 1964.

U.S. Office of Education. *Digest of Educational Statistics, 1963*. Washington: U.S. Government Printing Office, 1963.

————. *Digest of Educational Statistics, 1965 Edition*. Washington: U.S. Government Printing Office, 1965.

————. *Equality of Educational Opportunity*. Washington: U.S. Government Printing Office, 1966.

————. *Projections of Educational Statistics to 1973–74*. Washington: U.S. Government Printing Office, 1964.

————. *Projections of Educational Statistics to 1974–75*. Washington: U.S. Government Printing Office, 1965.

REPORTS

BLUMENFELD, WARREN S. *Some Characteristics of Finalists in the 1966 National Achievement Scholarship Program*. Evanston, Illinois: National Merit Scholarship Corporation, 1966.

College Board Score Reports: A Guide for Counselors. New York: College Entrance Examination Board, 1961.

College Board Score Reports. New York: College Entrance Examination Board, 1963.

College Entrance Examination Board. *Typical Student Budgets for College and Universities Participating in the College Scholarship Service During 1957–58*. New York: College Entrance Examination Board, 1959.

FIELDER, EARL R. *Student Expense Budgets of American Colleges and Universities for the 1965–66 Academic Year*, College Scholarship Service Technical Report, CSS 65-2. Princeton, N.J.: Educational Testing Service, 1965.

Ford Foundation, *Annual Reports*, 1961, 1962, 1963 and 1964. New York: Ford Foundation.

HALSEY, A. H., COCKCROFT, SIR JOHN, and SVENNILSON, INGVAR. *Higher Education and the Demand for Scientific Manpower in the United States.* Paris: Organisation for Economic Co-operation and Development, 1963.

HAVEN, ELIZABETH W., and SMITH, ROBERT E. *Financial Aid to College Students, 1963–64: Survey of Financial Aid Administered by Colleges and Universities to Full-Time Undergraduates*, Part I, Statistical Analysis Report SR-65-15, March 1965. Princeton, N.J.: Educational Testing Service.

MCKEE, RICHARD C. *College Aid for Students.* Health, Education and Welfare Indicators, July 1965. Washington: U.S. Government Printing Office.

———. *Financial Aid for College Students.* U.S. Office of Education. Washington: U.S. Government Printing Office, 1965.

NICHOLS, ROBERT C. *The Financial Status of Able Students.* Evanston, Illinois: National Merit Scholarship Corporation, 1965.

——— and ASTIN, ALEXANDER W. *Progress of the Merit Scholar: An Eight-Year Followup.* Evanston, Illinois: National Merit Scholarship Corporation, 1965.

Reports of the President of Harvard College, 1952–53 through 1964–65, Admission and Scholarship Committee Sections. Cambridge, Mass.: Harvard University, 1953–65.

ROBERTS, ROY J., and NICHOLS, ROBERT C. *Participants in the National Achievement Program for Negroes.* Evanston, Illinois: National Merit Scholarship Corporation, 1966.

SANDERS, J. EDWARD, and PALMER, HANS C. *The Financial Barrier to Higher Education in California: A Study Prepared for the California State Scholarship Commission.* Claremont, California: Pomona College, 1965.

WOLOZIN, HAROLD. *The Outlook for Higher Education.* Washington: Fund for the Advancement of Education, 1963.

ARTICLES AND PERIODICALS

ANGOFF, WILLIAM H. "The College Board SAT and the Superior Student," *The Superior Student*, Vol. 7, No. 2 (March–April 1965), pp. 10–15.

BOWEN, WILLIAM G. "University Finance in Britain and the United States: Implications of Financing Arrangements for Educational Issues," *Public Finance*, Vol. XVIII, No. 1 (1963), pp. 45–83.

BOWLES, FRANK H. "Contrasts in Education: Europe and the U.S.," *College Board Review*, Vol. 46 (Winter 1962), pp. 13–18.

BOWMAN, JAMES L. "Decisions and Diplomas," *American Education*, Vol. II, No. 5 (May 1966), pp. 30–32.

BUCK, PAUL H. "Balance in the College: A Chance to Restore an Old Ideal and Point a New Way," *Harvard Alumni Bulletin*, Vol. 48, No. 10 (Feb. 16, 1946), pp. 404–06.

———. "Who Comes to Harvard?" *Harvard Alumni Bulletin*, Vol. 50, No. 7 (January 10, 1948), pp. 313–17.

CARTTER, ALLAN M. "A New Look at the Supply of College Teachers," *Educational Record*, Vol. 46, No. 3 (Summer 1965), pp. 267–77.

———. "Economics of the University," *American Economic Review*, Vol. LV, No. 2 (May 1965), pp. 481–505.

——— and FARRELL, ROBERT. "Higher Education in the Last Third of the Century," *Educational Record*, Vol. 46, No. 2 (Spring 1965), pp. 119–28.

FITZWILLIAMS, JEANNETTE M. "Size Distribution of Income in 1963," *Survey of Current Business*, Office of Business Economics, Survey of Current Business, Vol. 44, No. 4 (April 1964), pp. 3–11.

GOLDSMITH, SELMA F. "Size Distribution of Personal Income," *Survey of Current Business*, Office of Business Economics, U.S. Department of Commerce, Vol. 38, No. 4 (April 1958), pp. 14–15.

HARRIS, SEYMOUR E. "Loaves and Fishes: Limited Aid Dollars Serving the Multitude," *Journal of the Association of College Admissions Counselors*, Vol. 9, No. 1 (Summer 1963), pp. 13–15.

JAFFE, A. J., and ADAMS, WALTER. "Trends in College Enrollment," *College Board Review*, No. 55 (Winter 1964–65), pp. 27–32.

MOON, REXFORD G., JR. "Determining Aid Needs for 1970: A Model," *College Board Review*, Vol. 54 (Fall 1964), pp. 11–13.

MONRO, JOHN U. "Capitalizing on the Federal Loans for Students," *College Board Review*, No. 37 (Winter 1959), pp. 12–17.

———. "Helping the Student to Help Himself," *College Board Review*, Summer 1952, pp. 351–57.

MORSE, JOHN F. "They Do Not Serve Who Only Stand and Wait," *Journal of the Association of College Admissions Counselors*, Vol. IX, No. 3 (Winter 1964), pp. 18–21.

NICHOLS, ROBERT C. "Career Decisions of Very Able Students," *Science*, Vol. 144 (June 12, 1964), pp. 1315–19.

PEARSON, RICHARD. "Liberal Arts Colleges and Universal Higher Education," *College Board Review*, No. 60 (Summer 1966), pp. 23–26.

RICKLEFS, ROGER. "Diverse Campuses," *Wall Street Journal*, May 18, 1966, pp. 1, 16.

SEIBEL, DEAN W. "Prediction of College Attendance," *Vocational Guidance Quarterly*, Summer 1963, pp. 265–72.

VANCE, STANLEY C. "Higher Education for the Executive Elite," *California Management Review*, Summer 1966, pp. 21–30.

UNPUBLISHED MATERIAL

CARTTER, ALLAN M. "Pricing Problems for Higher Education." Paper delivered at the College Scholarship Service Colloquium. Lake Geneva, Wisconsin: May 1966. (Mimeographed.)

GLIMP, FRED L. "Diversity, Financial Aid, and Institutional Pricing." Paper delivered at the College Scholarship Service Colloquium. Lake Geneva, Wisconsin: May 1966. (Typewritten.)

HAGE, ROBERT K. "Change and Challenges in Need Analysis." Address delivered to the 1961 Annual Meeting of the College Scholarship Service. New York: October 24, 1961. (Mimeographed.)

Harvard College, Office of Tests. *Performance of the Class of 1962 by Pre-Admission Information*. Cambridge, Mass.: Office of Tests, Harvard College, 1965. (Mimeographed.)

NORTH, WALTER M., and BROWN, KENNETH. *A General Survey of Student Assistance at Knox*. Office of Financial Aid, Knox College, Galesburg, Illinois, 1964. (Mimeographed.)

Name Index

Subject Index